Contents

How To Play

Winning Lines is the thrilling quiz game of general knowledge and numbers from the creators of *Who Wants To Be A Millionaire?* Now in *Winning Lines 2: The Quiz*, you can once again tackle those brain teasers from TV's top numbers show.

Fifteen brand new complete games of four rounds each, featuring the mind-tingling Wonderwall, plus the Memory Wonderwall, make for an exciting quiz book challenge. And the better your score, the better your imaginary holiday prize! Will it be Spaghetti Junction or are you good enough to make it around the world...?

Round One: The Winning Line

Use your number knowledge to answer each of these six questions. For bonus points, at the end of the round, add up your answers to see if they match the Winning Number to make up your **Winning Line**!

Round Two: Looking After Number One

Some of the answers to these ten questions will equal the Winning Number shown. It might be as many as ten or as few as one. Take your time – there's no time limit on this round – because to score any points here, you must select all questions which match exactly the Winning Number.

Round Three: Wonderwall

We hope the number work-outs in the previous two rounds have limbered you up for this general knowledge challenge. You've got three minutes to search out the 20 answers hidden in the Wonderwall. Narrow your selection by crossing off the answers as you go. Right, pencils ready...?

Round Four: Memory Wonderwall

There are only ten questions here but they're not for the faint-hearted! You'll first see ten numbered answers on the Memory Wonderwall. You've got **one minute** to memorise both the number and the answer. Then turn the page to answer ten questions from memory. Score double points if you can remember both the answer and corresponding number from the wall.

The Scorecard

At the end of each game, there's a scorecard for you to add up your score. All the answers are at the back of the book. Once you've determined your total score, flip to the Winning Lines Holiday Prize Table on the page opposite to see how glamorous an imaginary holiday you have won!

Holiday Prize Table

SCORE	DESTINATION
1 – 2	Spaghetti Junction
3 – 4	London Theatre
5 – 6	Scottish Castle
7 – 8	Ireland
9 – 18	Amsterdam
19 – 20	Paris
21 – 22	Monte Carlo
23 – 24	Majorca
25 – 26	Italian Lakes
27 – 28	New York
29 – 30	Hong Kong
31 – 32	USA
33 – 34	Mauritius
35 – 36	Caribbean Cruise
37 – 38	African Safari
39 – 42	Florida
43 – 46	Hawaii
47 – 50	Barbados
51 – 54	Australia & The Barrier Reef
55 – 58	Round the World!

GAME ONE

Answers for Game One on page 156. Scorecard page 15.

1 The Winning Line

HOW TO PLAY

First answer the following six questions in the spaces provided (Tip! Answers will be a number). Transfer your answers to the oval spaces in the Winning Line. If these answers add up to the winning number, you have a Winning Line! There is no time limit for this round.

1 How many 50 pence coins are equal in value to thirty-five 10 pence coins?

2 If the Beatles had had one more guitarist, how many members of the band would there have been?

3 If there were one less ring on the Olympic flag, how many rings would there be?

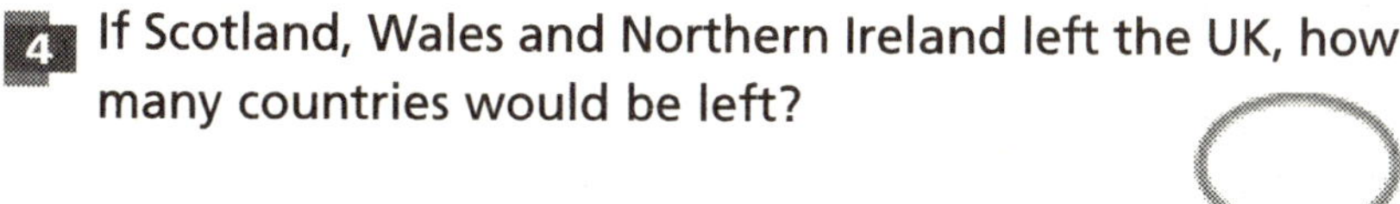

4 If Scotland, Wales and Northern Ireland left the UK, how many countries would be left?

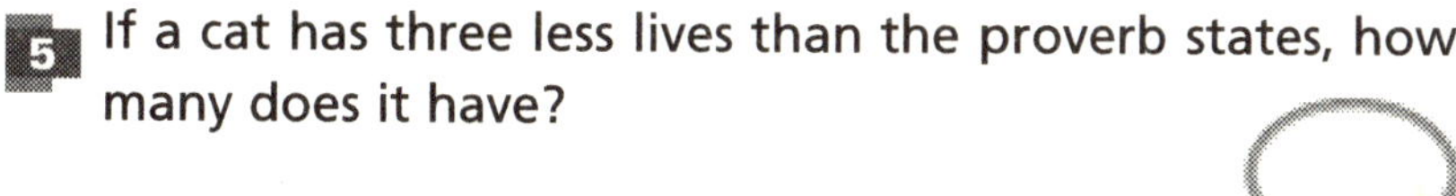

5 If a cat has three less lives than the proverb states, how many does it have?

6 If one of the legs was missing from the flag of the Isle of Man, how many would it have?

Create your Winning Line:

◯ + ◯ + ◯ + ◯ + ◯ + ◯

= Winning Number = 25

SCORING

Score one point for each question answered correctly, plus an additional two points if your answers successfully add up to the Winning Number.

2 Looking After Number One

HOW TO PLAY

Look at the following ten questions. Tick only those questions whose answers correspond with the winning number shown in the oval below the questions. There is no time limit for this round.

For example, if the Winning Number = 7

How many dwarfs lived with Snow White?

1 What number shirt is usually worn by the scrum half in rugby union?

2 How many operas comprise Richard Wagner's 'Ring Cycle'?

3 Traditionally, how many legs does a milking stool have?

4 How many atoms of hydrogen combine with one atom of oxygen to form one molecule of water?

5 How many does it 'take to tango'?

6 How many English counties border Wales?

7 How many sons did Ma Boswell have in the TV sitcom 'Bread'?

8 How many forenames does the politician Michael Portillo have?

9 In total, how many stripes does a police sergeant have on both his sleeves?

10 A candidate in a British General Election will lose their deposit if they do not receive more than what percentage of the votes cast?

WINNING NUMBER = 4

SCORING

Score ten points if your answers match exactly with those in the back of the book.

3 Wonderwall

13 William	34 Leopard		28 Lion
5 Puma		29 Henry	
32 Tia Maria	40 Russian		
10 Liver		11 Red	
19 Swiss	14 Polish		30 Eye
45 Advocaat		22 Heart	
1 Tiger	15 Edward		48 Ear
26 Rat		25 Austrian	
44 Dee	7 Mouse		33 Don
18 Panther		2 Arbroath	

1. Which Scottish football club plays its home matches at Pittodrie Stadium?
2. Which member of the cat family has the Latin name Panthera pardus?
3. In judo, what colour belt does a beginner wear?
4. The adjective 'hepatic' relates to which organ of the human body?
5. What was the first name of Mr Wordsworth, the Poet Laureate between 1843-50?
6. Which sea washes the western shoreline of Saudi Arabia?
7. Which Scottish town or city stands at the northern end of the M90 motorway?
8. Which river flows through Stoke, Nottingham and Newark?
9. Which liqueur is added to vodka and orange juice to make a 'Harvey Wallbanger'?
10. What nationality was the composer Frederic Chopin at birth?

HOW TO PLAY AND SCORING

The answers to the questions are in the Wonderwall below. Write the number of your answer in the space provided, crossing answers off the Wall as you go. The time limit is 3 minutes. One point for each correct answer.

3 Snake
43 Green
20 Inverness
42 Tornado
49 Harrier
21 Derwent
12 Benedictine
46 Trent
36 Brain
35 Slovakian
27 Yellow
23 Vole
24 Hercules
8 Dundee
38 Mink
37 Black
17 White
16 Galliano
31 Philip
41 Aberdeen
47 Nimrod
6 Cointreau
4 Perth
39 Avon
9 Tucano

11 ◯ Which hand-held device is used to move a cursor on a computer screen?

12 ◯ Which RAF aircraft is sometimes referred to as a 'jump jet'?

13 ◯ Which type of roll consists of a rectangular sponge spread with jam and cream and rolled up into a cylinder?

14 ◯ A member of the 7th Armoured Division in the British Army is sometimes referred to as a Desert ...?

15 ◯ What is the surname of the winner of the celebrity 'Big Brother' held in conjunction with Comic Relief in 2001?

16 ◯ Which Dutchman became the Director of Football at Glasgow Rangers in December 2001?

17 ◯ Which animal always appears at the start of an MGM film?

18 ◯ According to Genesis, who was a great grandson of Noah and famed for being a mighty hunter?

19 ◯ Feargal Sharkey had a UK No 1 single in 1985 with 'A Good ...'?

20 ◯ What was the real first name of the jazz pianist Duke Ellington?

4 Memory Wonderwall

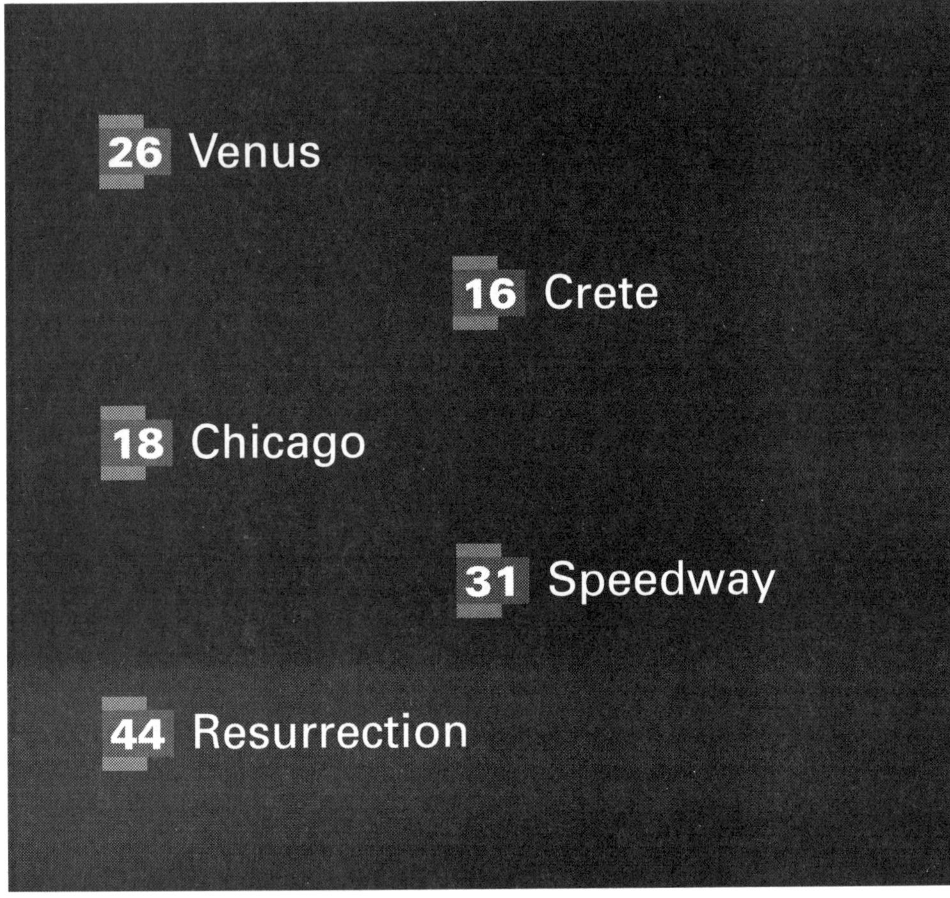

HOW TO PLAY

You have one minute to memorise the mini Wonderwall! Memorise both the word answer and its corresponding number. Then turn the page to answer the ten questions from memory.

FOR EXAMPLE

Question: What is the capital of Iceland?

Answer: 11. Reykjavik (*Scores 2 points*)

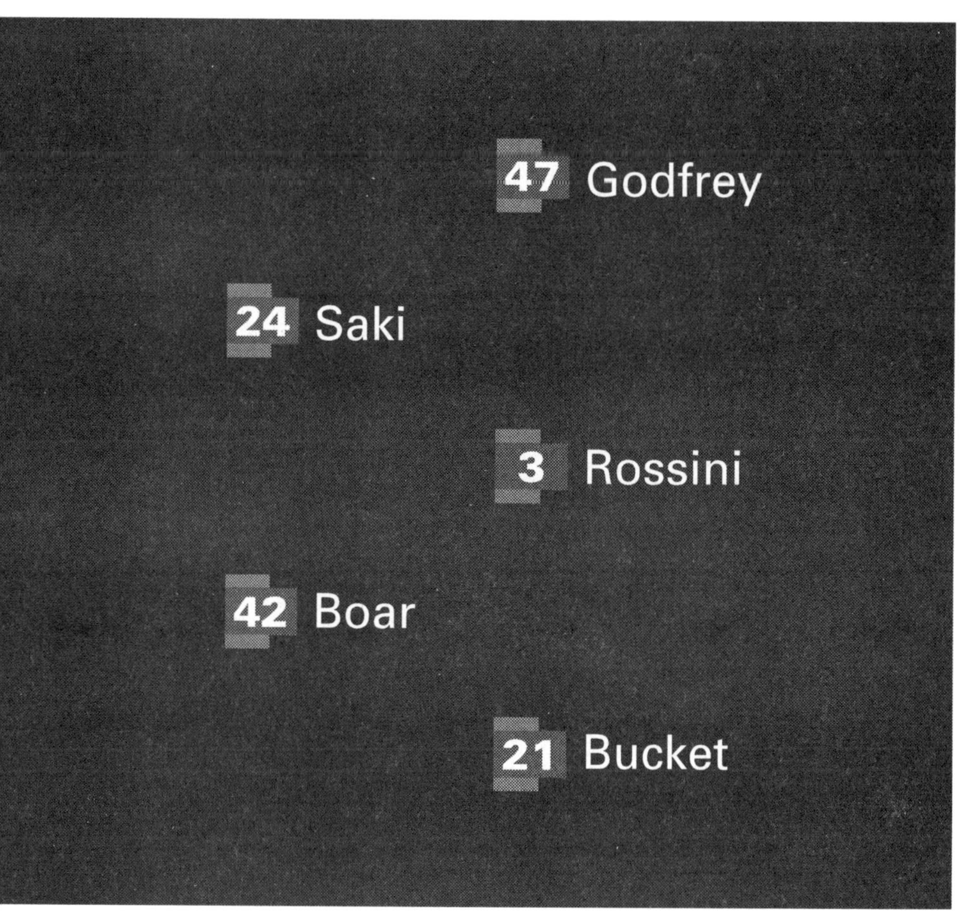

SCORING

Award yourself one point for answering the question correctly, and a bonus point for remembering the number that corresponds to your answer.

Turn page for questions

Round 4: Memory Wonderwall Questions

1. Which US city is the eastern terminus of the famous Route 66?

2. In which sport was New Zealand's Ivan Mauger a six-times world champion?

3. Which character in 'Dad's Army' was played by Arnold Ridley?

4. Which planet in our solar system is nearest in size to the Earth?

5. On which Mediterranean island was the Minoan civilization established?

6. What word accompanies 'Alien', to give the title of the fourth film in that series starring Sigourney Weaver?

7. What was the pseudonym of Hector Hugh Munro?

8. Who wrote the opera 'William Tell'?

9. What is a male badger called?

10. The Asian style of cuisine known as 'Balti' takes its name from the Urdu for what?

Scorecard

Answers for Game One are on page 156.

ROUND 1: THE WINNING LINE

Number of correct answers ---------

Add 2 points for creating the Winning Line ---------

(Maximum Score = 8) **Your Score**

ROUND 2: LOOKING AFTER NUMBER ONE

(Your score will be either 0 or 10) **Your Score**

ROUND 3: WONDERWALL

(Maximum Score = 20) **Your Score**

ROUND 4: MEMORY WONDERWALL

(Maximum Score = 20) **Your Score**

TOTAL SCORE

HOLIDAY SCORE

Go to the Holiday Prize Table on page 5 to find out whether your total score will take you around the world!

GAME TWO

Answers for Game Two on page 156. Scorecard page 25.

1 The Winning Line

HOW TO PLAY

First answer the following six questions in the spaces provided (Tip! Answers will be a number). Transfer your answers to the oval spaces in the Winning Line. If these answers add up to the winning number, you have a Winning Line! There is no time limit for this round.

1. How many people would it take to form four teams in a three-legged race?

2. If you add the number of Shakespeare's 'Gentlemen of Verona' to the number of witches in 'Macbeth', how many people would you have?

3. If you have fired one bullet out of each of your three fully loaded six-shooters, how many rounds do you have left?

4 If the original gang who founded the SDP in 1981 had been double the size, how many members would there have been?

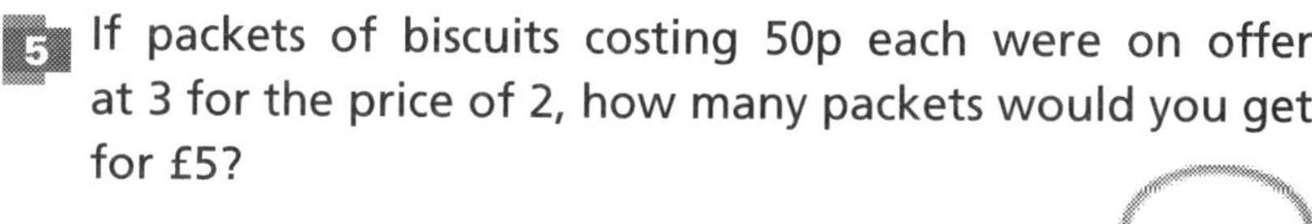

5 If packets of biscuits costing 50p each were on offer at 3 for the price of 2, how many packets would you get for £5?

6 How many different vowels are in the place name 'Enniskillen'?

Create your Winning Line:

( ) + ( ) + ( ) + ( ) + ( ) + ( )

= Winning Number = 53

SCORING

Score one point for each question answered correctly, plus an additional two points if your answers successfully add up to the Winning Number.

2 Looking After Number One

HOW TO PLAY

Look at the following ten questions. Tick only those questions whose answers correspond with the winning number shown in the oval below the questions. There is no time limit for this round.

For example, if the Winning Number = 7

How many dwarfs lived with Snow White?

1 How many Olympic gold medals has Daley Thompson won?

2 How many 'Goodies' were there in the TV comedy series of the same name?

3 Between them, how many wheels do two unicycles have?

4 How many blind mice ran after the farmer's wife, according to the nursery rhyme?

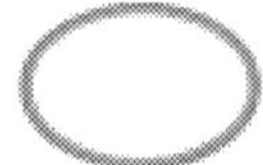

5 What is the number of the TV channel known as Sianel Pedwar Cymru in Wales?

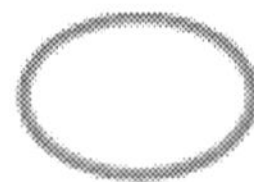

6 In pennies, what is the value of the British coin that has the Prince of Wales' feathers on its reverse?

7 How many times can a horse win the Epsom Derby?

8 How many 'Little Boys' did Rolf Harris sing about in his 1969 UK No 1 single?

9 How many teaspoonfuls are equivalent to one tablespoonful?

10 In 1998, how many member states of the EU decided not to enter the first round of EMU and adopt the Euro?

WINNING NUMBER =

SCORING

Score ten points if your answers match exactly with those in the back of the book.

3 Wonderwall

13 Wagner	34 Jupiter	28 Rome
5 Harriott	29 Mercury	
32 Indiana	40 Rum	
10 Swan	11 Tennessee	
19 Gold	14 Dove	30 Mars
45 London	22 Vodka	
1 Emerald	15 Saxophone	48 Trombone
26 Crow	25 Cornet	
44 Tin	7 Melbourne	33 Whisky
18 Copper	2 Trumpet	

1. Which planet in our solar system has a feature known as the 'Great Red Spot'?
2. Which chemical element has the symbol Ag?
3. The author of 'Call of the Wild' and 'White Fang' was Jack ...?
4. Who, in 1880, composed the '1812 Overture'?
5. Which Jamie came to fame as television's 'Naked Chef'?
6. According to the Bible, which was the first bird released from the Ark by Noah?
7. Of which alcoholic drink is Bacardi a famous brand?
8. With which instrument is Glenn Miller chiefly associated?
9. Which state of the USA shares its name with one of the five Great Lakes of North America?
10. According to the song title, which precious stone is 'a girl's best friend'?

HOW TO PLAY AND SCORING

The answers to the questions are in the Wonderwall below. Write the number of your answer in the space provided, crossing answers off the Wall as you go. The time limit is 3 minutes. One point for each correct answer.

3 Silver
43 Rankin
20 Schubert
42 Brandy
49 Sapphire
21 Saturn
12 Sydney
46 Oliver
36 Clarinet
35 Port
27 Mississippi
23 Paris
24 Diamond
8 Minnesota
38 Tchaikovsky
37 Lawson
17 Turner
16 Ruby
31 Eagle
41 Michigan
47 Raven
6 Brahms
4 Beethoven
39 Neptune
9 Aluminium

11 ( ) Who painted 'The Fighting Téméraire' and 'Rain, Steam and Speed'?

12 ( ) What name is given to a cone-shaped wafer biscuit, especially one filled with ice cream?

13 ( ) The name of which metal is used as a slang term for a policeman?

14 ( ) The plays 'Cat on a Hot Tin Roof' and 'A Streetcar Named Desire' were written by ... Williams?

15 ( ) What name was given to a St Bernard dog in the title of a 1992 film and its subsequent sequels?

16 ( ) Which Roman god was identified with the Greek god Poseidon?

17 ( ) Which city hosted the 1956 Summer Olympic Games?

18 ( ) Which character did Joanna Lumley play opposite David McCallum as 'Steel', in a TV series of the 1970s and 80s?

19 ( ) A nickname given to Queen Anne was '... Nan'?

20 ( ) The Australian city of Perth stands on which river?

4 Memory Wonderwall

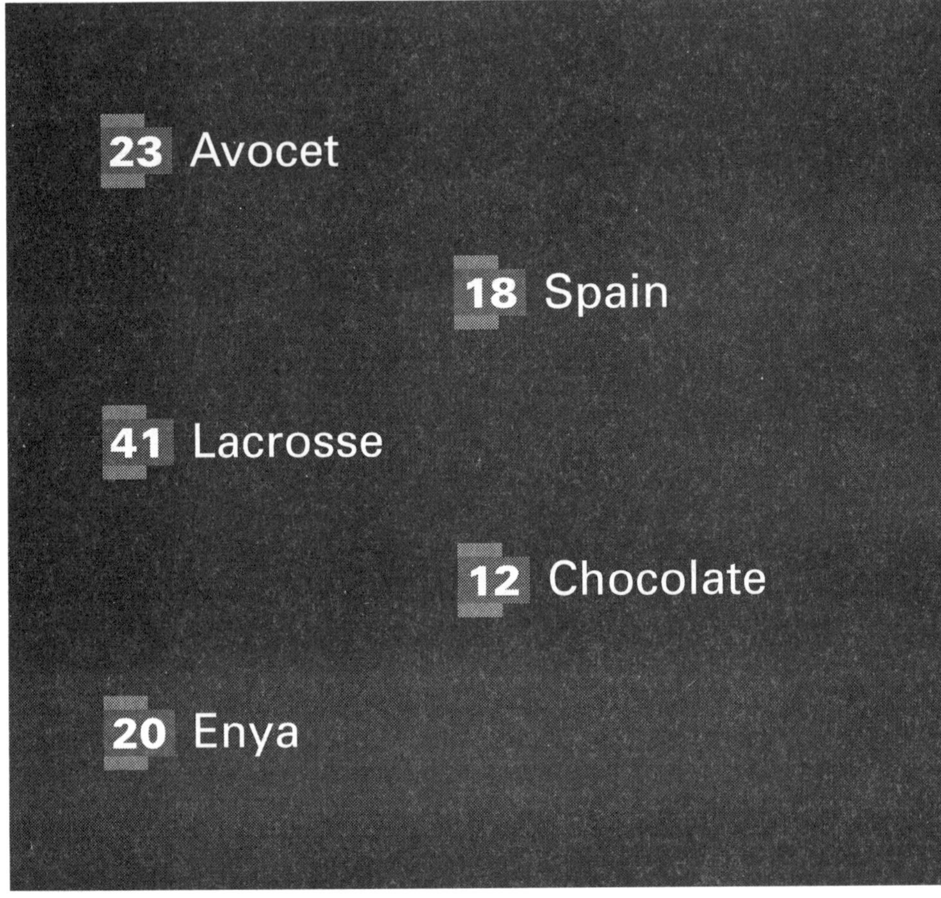

HOW TO PLAY

You have one minute to memorise the mini Wonderwall! Memorise both the word answer and its corresponding number. Then turn the page to answer the ten questions from memory.

FOR EXAMPLE

Question: What is the capital of Iceland?

Answer: 11. Reykjavik (*Scores 2 points)*

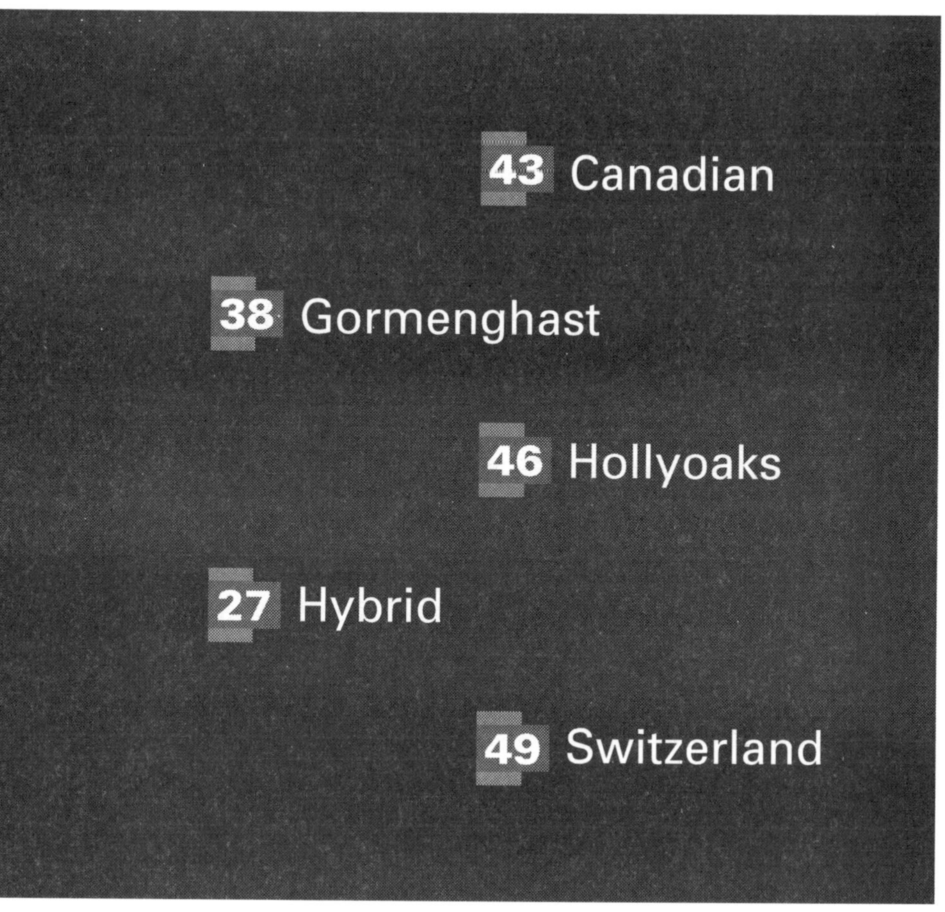

SCORING

Award yourself one point for answering the question correctly, and a bonus point for remembering the number that corresponds to your answer.

Turn page for questions

Round 4: Memory Wonderwall Questions

1. What name is given to the type of computer that has both digital and analogue components?

2. What nationality is Mike Myers, star of the 'Wayne's World' and 'Austin Powers' films?

3. Which bird is the symbol of the Royal Society for the Protection of Birds?

4. Carob is a low-fat, low-calorie, low-caffeine alternative to what?

5. In which sport is the Iroquois Cup competed for?

6. 'Orinoco Flow' was a 1988 UK No 1 single for which artist?

7. In which country is the Romansch language spoken?

8. Which castle is home to the Earls of Groan in Mervyn Peake's novels?

9. Which country fought the War of Jenkins' Ear against Britain?

10. In which TV soap have Les Hunter, Izzy Cornwell and Zara Morgan been characters?

Scorecard

Answers for Game Two are on page 156.

ROUND 1: THE WINNING LINE

Number of correct answers ---------

Add 2 points for creating the Winning Line ---------

(Maximum Score = 8) **Your Score**

ROUND 2: LOOKING AFTER NUMBER ONE

(Your score will be either 0 or 10) **Your Score**

ROUND 3: WONDERWALL

(Maximum Score = 20) **Your Score**

ROUND 4: MEMORY WONDERWALL

(Maximum Score = 20) **Your Score**

TOTAL SCORE

HOLIDAY SCORE

Go to the Holiday Prize Table on page 5 to find out whether your total score will take you around the world!

GAME THREE

Answers for Game Three on page 156. Scorecard page 35.

1 The Winning Line

HOW TO PLAY

First answer the following six questions in the spaces provided (Tip! Answers will be a number). Transfer your answers to the oval spaces in the Winning Line. If these answers add up to the winning number, you have a Winning Line! There is no time limit for this round.

1 How many players would be left in a rugby union team if some of them went off to form an indoor volleyball team?

2 If a professional boxing match is stopped after six rounds, how many minutes has the fight lasted?

3 In Roman numerals, if you divide M by C, what number are you left with in Arabic numerals?

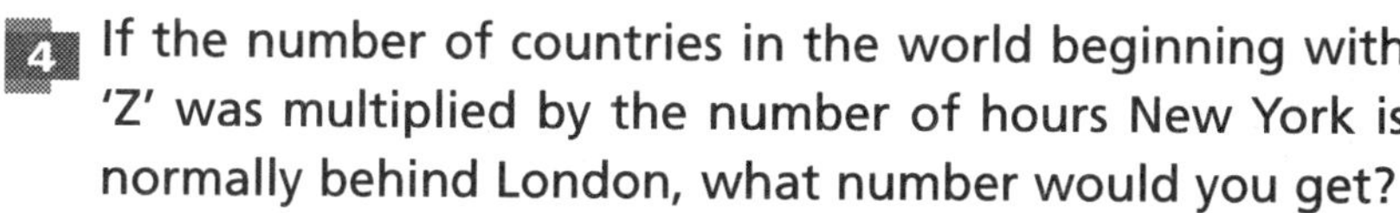

4 If the number of countries in the world beginning with 'Z' was multiplied by the number of hours New York is normally behind London, what number would you get?

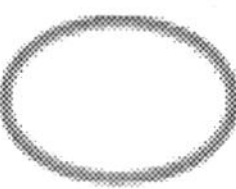

5 On a chessboard, if half the white squares were coloured black, how many white ones would there be left?

6 If you received 20p for every contestant on William G Stewart's quiz programme, how many pounds would you have?

Create your Winning Line:

+ + + + +

= Winning Number = 66

SCORING

Score one point for each question answered correctly, plus an additional two points if your answers successfully add up to the Winning Number.

2 Looking After Number One

HOW TO PLAY

Look at the following ten questions. Tick only those questions whose answers correspond with the winning number shown in the oval below the questions. There is no time limit for this round.

For example, if the Winning Number = 7

How many dwarfs lived with Snow White?

1 What is the maximum score that may be awarded by a judge to a competitor in international gymnastics?

2 What number appeared in the title of the 1979 film starring Dudley Moore, Julie Andrews and Bo Derek?

3 How many miles are there in one league?

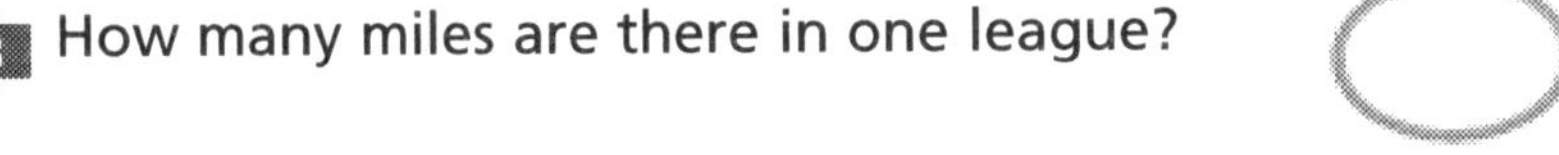

4 In 1752, how many days were lost when the Gregorian calendar superseded the Julian calendar in England?

5 The prefix 'deci' indicates something has been divided by what number?

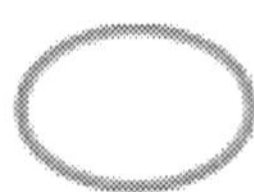

6 How many fluid ounces are there in half a British pint?

7 According to the Bible, how many 'Tribes of Israel' were there, each descended from a son of Jacob?

8 What number completes the name of the ancient board game popular with shepherds, '...Men's Morris'?

9 At what number on the Beaufort Scale is a wind first classed as a hurricane?

10 In monetary slang, how many pounds is a 'pony' worth?

WINNING NUMBER = 

SCORING

Score ten points if your answers match exactly with those in the back of the book.

3 Wonderwall

13 Assam
34 Skipjack
28 Blue
5 Peru
29 Albatross
32 Brazil
40 Gemini
10 Castle
11 Formosa
19 China
14 Frankenstein
30 Hawk
45 India
22 Corporal
1 Silk
15 Major
48 Argentina
26 Sergeant
25 Dracula
44 Green
7 Mercury
33 Zombies
18 Chile
2 Skylab

1 By what crime-fighting name is Dick Grayson, friend of superhero Bruce Wayne, also known?

2 What was the former name of Sri Lanka?

3 Which chess piece is known in Germany as 'Springer'?

4 Which South American country completes the title of the 1978 film in which Gregory Peck played a renegade Nazi, 'The Boys from ...'?

5 Which supernatural character was created by Bram Stoker?

6 Which amphibian shares its name with part of a horse's hoof?

7 What name is given to the soft downy covering on a deer's antlers whilst they are growing?

8 Which NASA programme took Armstong and Aldrin to the Moon in 1969?

9 Which colour is traditionally associated with the British Conservative Party?

10 Which army rank completes the title of the first 'Carry On' film, 'Carry On ...'?

HOW TO PLAY AND SCORING

The answers to the questions are in the Wonderwall below. Write the number of your answer in the space provided, crossing answers off the Wall as you go. The time limit is 3 minutes. One point for each correct answer.

3 Colonel
43 Yellow
20 Falcon
42 Velvet
49 Salamander
21 Orange
12 Newt
46 Ceylon
36 Bishop
35 Apollo
27 Hermes
23 Frog
24 Cotton
8 Mummies
38 Toad
37 Denim
17 Red
16 Rook
31 Ecuador
41 Werewolf
47 Eagle
6 King
4 Robin
39 Knight
9 Damask

11 ( ) The name of which eastern country is used as Cockney rhyming slang for a mate?

12 ( ) Which type of creature is Ken Livingstone famed for keeping?

13 ( ) From which country did Paddington Bear arrive in England?

14 ( ) What term is used for the completion of a hole in golf in two strokes below par?

15 ( ) What word describes punishment in which physical pain is inflicted on the body?

16 ( ) Astrologically speaking, which sign is known as 'The Twins'?

17 ( ) Which pop group had a hit single in 1964 with 'She's Not There'?

18 ( ) The North American name for candy floss is ' ... candy'?

19 ( ) According to the saying, what colour rag is it best not to wave at a bull?

20 ( ) Which British Transport Minister introduced the Breathalyser in 1967?

4 Memory Wonderwall

41 Scurvy

27 USA

15 Mauritius

36 Llewelyn

8 Everton

HOW TO PLAY

You have one minute to memorise the mini Wonderwall! Memorise both the word answer and its corresponding number. Then turn the page to answer the ten questions from memory.

FOR EXAMPLE

Question: What is the capital of Iceland?

Answer: 11. Reykjavik (*Scores 2 points*)

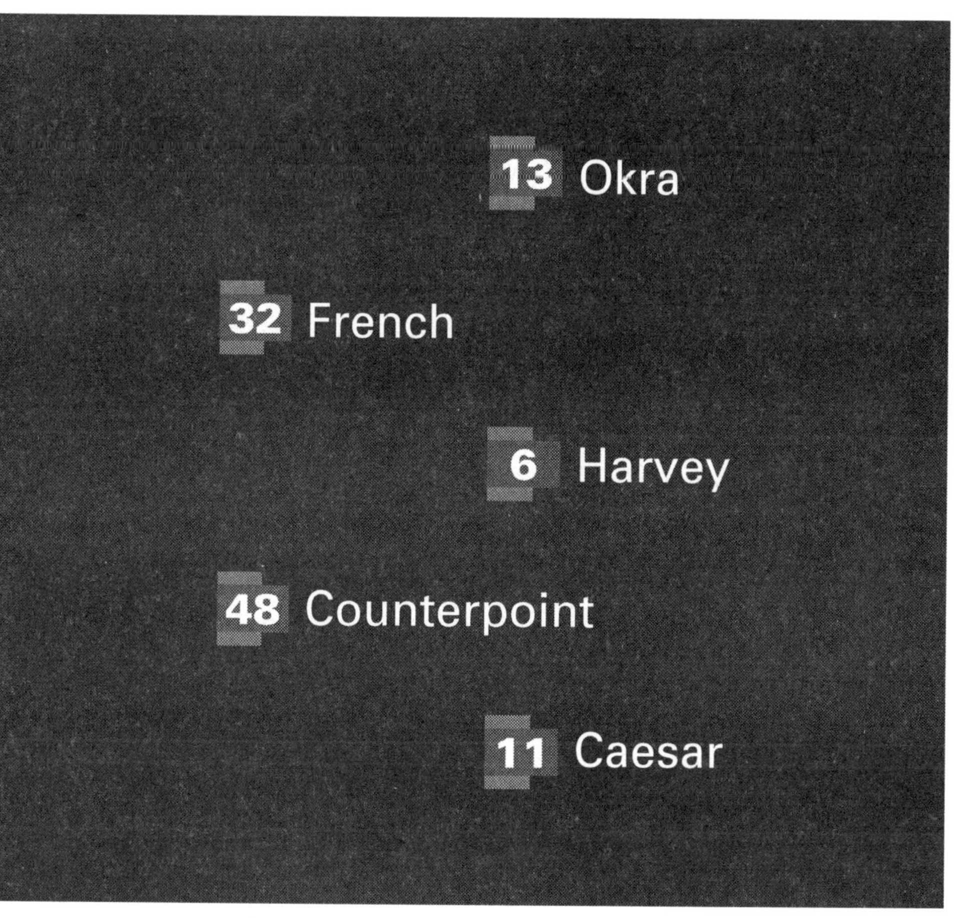

SCORING

Award yourself one point for answering the question correctly, and a bonus point for remembering the number that corresponds to your answer.

Turn page for questions

Round 4: Memory Wonderwall Questions

1 The Russian title 'Tsar' is derived from the name of which older title?

2 Natives of Puerto Rico are citizens of which country?

3 Who is the giant rabbit friend of Elwood P Dowd?

4 What nationality was the composer Hector Berlioz?

5 What is the title of the long-running music quiz on BBC Radio 4 hosted by Ned Sherrin?

6 The dodo was native to which island?

7 Which disease is caused by a deficiency of vitamin C?

8 When founded in 1878, which English football club was called St Domingo FC?

9 What was the surname of the actor who played 'Q' in the James Bond films?

10 Which vegetable is popularly known as 'ladies' fingers'?

Scorecard

Answers for Game Three are on page 156.

ROUND 1: THE WINNING LINE

Number of correct answers ---------

Add 2 points for creating the Winning Line ---------

(Maximum Score = 8) **Your Score**

ROUND 2: LOOKING AFTER NUMBER ONE
(Your score will be either 0 or 10) **Your Score**

ROUND 3: WONDERWALL
(Maximum Score = 20) **Your Score**

ROUND 4: MEMORY WONDERWALL
(Maximum Score = 20) **Your Score**

TOTAL SCORE

HOLIDAY SCORE

Go to the Holiday Prize Table on page 5 to find out whether your total score will take you around the world!

Game Four

Answers for Game Four on page 157. Scorecard page 45.

1 The Winning Line

HOW TO PLAY

First answer the following six questions in the spaces provided (Tip! Answers will be a number). Transfer your answers to the oval spaces in the Winning Line. If these answers add up to the winning number, you have a Winning Line! There is no time limit for this round.

1 If a British man is eligible for his state pension in thirty years time, how old is he now?

2 How many points in total are scored for a try in rugby union and a touchdown in American football?

3 11 years ago, you passed your driving test on the day it was legal for you to drive a car on British roads. How old are you now?

4 What do you get if you add the number of ghosts who appear to Ebenezer Scrooge, to the number of colours on the flag of France?

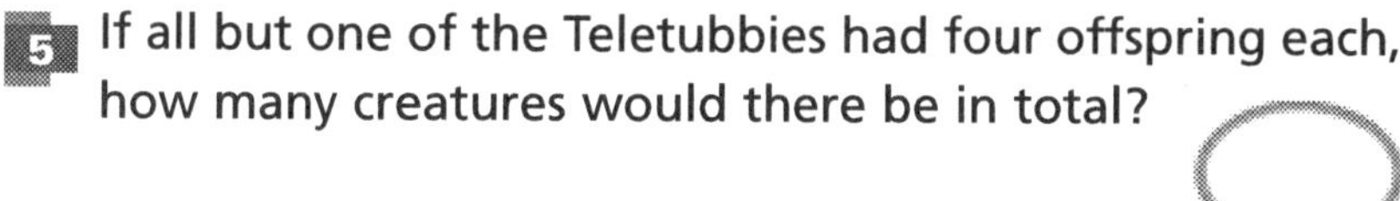

5 If all but one of the Teletubbies had four offspring each, how many creatures would there be in total?

6 Two popes have been called John Paul: what number is obtained by adding their regnal numbers together?

Create your Winning Line:

+ + + + +

SCORING

Score one point for each question answered correctly, plus an additional two points if your answers successfully add up to the Winning Number.

2 Looking After Number One

HOW TO PLAY

Look at the following ten questions. Tick only those questions whose answers correspond with the winning number shown in the oval below the questions. There is no time limit for this round.

For example, if the Winning Number = 7

How many dwarfs lived with Snow White?

1 If you make a snooker break of red, brown, red, green, red, pink, red, blue: how many points have you scored?

2 A fast talker traditionally talks at how many 'to the dozen'?

3 If you celebrated your crystal wedding anniversary six years ago, how many years have you been married?

4 On the 24 hour clock, how many 'hundred hours' is 8 o'clock in the evening?

5 How many pairs of chromosomes does a normal healthy human have in each cell?

6 Queen Elizabeth II was born in 19...?

7 What number, when repeated, denotes normal vision?

8 Which position in our alphabet does the letter 'S' occupy?

9 How many thousand 'Leagues under the Sea' did Jules Verne write about in 1869?

10 What perfect score is aimed for when playing Blackjack or Pontoon?

WINNING NUMBER = 

SCORING

Score ten points if your answers match exactly with those in the back of the book.

3 Wonderwall

13 Canberra	34 Balthazar	28 Poison
5 Opium	29 Shylock	
32 Rook	40 Crow	
10 Super	11 Chandler	
19 Jeroboam	14 Timon	30 Thames
45 Singular	22 Canary	
1 Obsession	15 Synthetic	48 Cleopatra
26 Gill	25 Caesar	
44 Adelaide	7 Forth	33 Butcher
18 Methuselah	2 White	

1. Which champagne bottle holds the equivalent of twenty standard bottles?
2. Which unit of liquid imperial measurement is equal to two pints?
3. Which Australian city was renamed in 1911 after a famous 19th century British scientist?
4. Which perfume was launched by Christian Dior in 1985?
5. Which Shakespeare character is 'the Moor of Venice'?
6. Which shipping area is named after a river that rises in the Cotswolds?
7. What does the 'S' stand for in the acronym 'LASER'?
8. What is the predominant colour of the first choice shirts of the French national rugby union team?
9. According to the poem by Edgar Allen Poe, which bird said 'Nevermore'?
10. Which 'Fabulous Boys' did Jeff and Beau Bridges play in a 1989 film?

HOW TO PLAY AND SCORING

The answers to the questions are in the Wonderwall below. Write the number of your answer in the space provided, crossing answers off the Wall as you go. The time limit is 3 minutes. One point for each correct answer.

3 Bushel
43 Cooper
20 Yellow
42 Peck
49 Cairns
21 Othello
12 Gallon
46 Shannon
36 Black
35 Quart
27 Darwin
23 Bailey
24 Raven
8 Red
38 Stimulated
37 Nebuchadnezzar
17 Baker
16 Eden
31 Blue
41 Strategic
47 Magpie
6 Rehoboam
4 Hobart
39 Tweed
9 Tyne

11 What sort of 'car' did Mike Mercury pilot in the early Gerry Anderson puppet series?

12 According to the Old Testament, who lived to be 969 years old?

13 Which American novelist created the detective Philip Marlowe?

14 Which sea washes the shores of China and Korea?

15 Which cruise liner was used as a troop ship during the Falklands War?

16 Who had UK hit singles in 1961 with 'Hats Off To Larry' and 'Runaway'?

17 Which river forms part of the border between England and Scotland?

18 Newcastle United and Notts County are both nicknamed after which bird?

19 After whom are two needles named, one in Central Park, New York and the other on the Embankment in London?

20 Through which respiratory organ does a fish obtain oxygen from water?

4 Memory Wonderwall

HOW TO PLAY

You have one minute to memorise the mini Wonderwall! Memorise both the word answer and its corresponding number. Then turn the page to answer the ten questions from memory.

FOR EXAMPLE

Question: What is the capital of Iceland?

Answer: 11. Reykjavik *(Scores 2 points)*

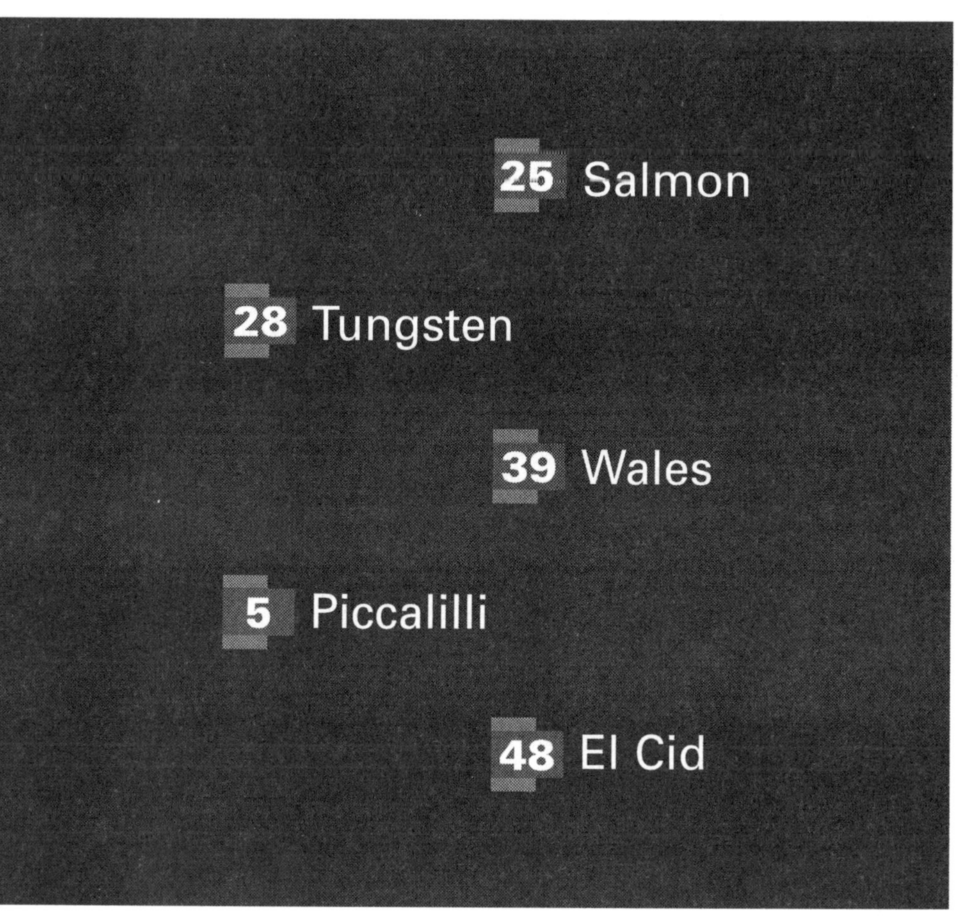

SCORING

Award yourself one point for answering the question correctly, and a bonus point for remembering the number that corresponds to your answer.

Turn page for questions

Round 4: Memory Wonderwall Questions

1 Who were England's first opponents in an international rugby union match at Twickenham?

2 Which bird was 'Pretty' according to the 1966 UK No 1 single for Manfred Mann?

3 Which sea separates Australia and New Zealand?

4 By what name is Rodrigo Diaz de Vivar better known?

5 W is the chemical symbol for which element?

6 For her role in which film did Whoopi Goldberg win the 1990 Best Supporting Actress Oscar?

7 What is the name of the witch, played by Alyson Hannigan, in TV's 'Buffy the Vampire Slayer'?

8 Sockeye is a variety of which fish?

9 What general name is given to the bright yellow mixture of cauliflower, gherkins and onions in a mustard vinegar?

10 In 'Peter Pan', what is Wendy's surname?

Scorecard

Answers for Game Four are on page 157.

ROUND 1: THE WINNING LINE

Number of correct answers ---------

Add 2 points for creating the Winning Line ---------

(Maximum Score = 8) **Your Score**

ROUND 2: LOOKING AFTER NUMBER ONE
(Your score will be either 0 or 10) **Your Score**

ROUND 3: WONDERWALL
(Maximum Score = 20) **Your Score**

ROUND 4: MEMORY WONDERWALL
(Maximum Score = 20) **Your Score**

TOTAL SCORE

HOLIDAY SCORE

Go to the Holiday Prize Table on page 5 to find out whether your total score will take you around the world!

GAME FIVE

Answers for Game Five on page 157. Scorecard page 55.

1 The Winning Line

HOW TO PLAY

First answer the following six questions in the spaces provided (Tip! Answers will be a number). Transfer your answers to the oval spaces in the Winning Line. If these answers add up to the winning number, you have a Winning Line! There is no time limit for this round.

1 If Eddie Cochran had taken one more 'Step to Heaven' in his only UK No 1 hit, how many would he have taken?

2 If the number on the door of the Chancellor of the Exchequer's official London residence was four less, what would it be?

3 If four events were removed from the decathlon, how many would be left?

4 If the emergency telephone number for the police in the UK was divided by 111, what would it be?

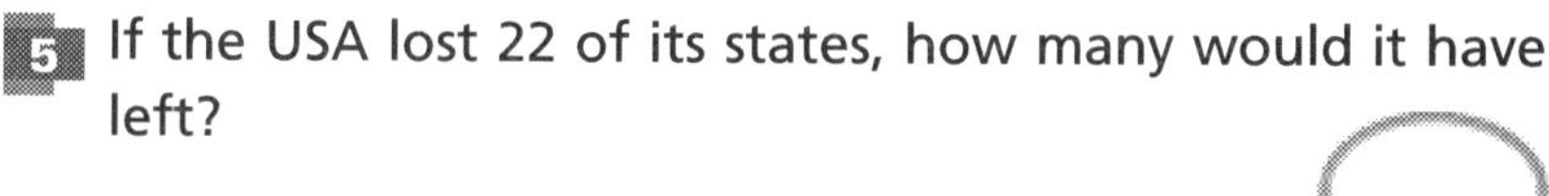

5 If the USA lost 22 of its states, how many would it have left?

6 If you answer a question every 5 seconds, how many would you answer in $1\frac{1}{2}$ minutes?

Create your Winning Line:

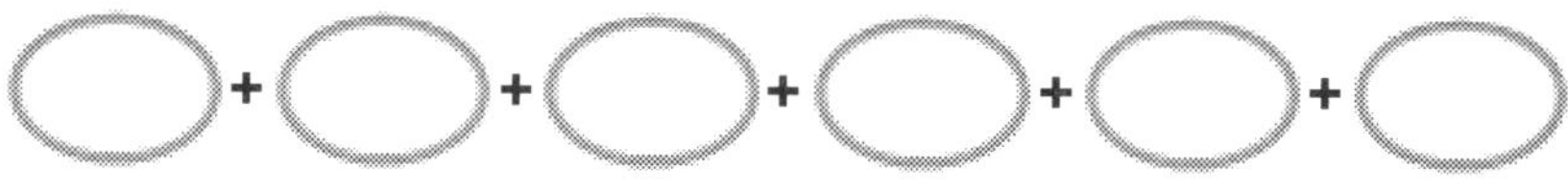

= Winning Number =

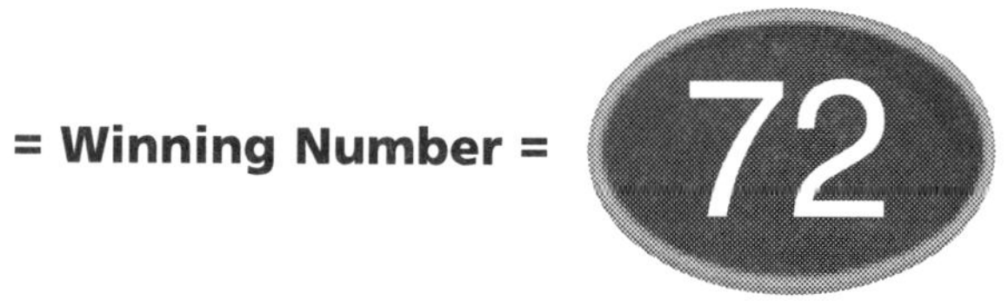

SCORING

Score one point for each question answered correctly, plus an additional two points if your answers successfully add up to the Winning Number.

2 Looking After Number One

HOW TO PLAY

Look at the following ten questions. Tick only those questions whose answers correspond with the winning number shown in the oval below the questions. There is no time limit for this round.

For example, if the Winning Number = 7

How many dwarfs lived with Snow White?

1 How many laps of the track does an athlete complete during a major 10,000 metres race?

2 To the nearest hour, how many hours does it take the Earth to make one complete revolution on its axis?

3 On what date in March does Lady Day fall?

4 When repeated, what number was part of the title of a 1969 UK No 1 single for Zager and Evans?

5 What is the minimum age at which a person is eligible to become a Member of Parliament at Westminster?

6 What number might be referred to as 'Two Little Ducks' in Bingo?

7 Charles Lindbergh made his famous solo transatlantic flight in 19...?

8 How many tiles are there in a standard set of 6-spot dominoes?

9 In the Revised Standard Version of the Bible, which number psalm begins 'The Lord is my shepherd I shall not want...'?

10 On which date in December does the day before Boxing Day fall?

WINNING NUMBER = 

SCORING

Score ten points if your answers match exactly with those in the back of the book.

3 Wonderwall

13 Capri
34 Aardvark
28 September
5 Floyd
29 Cortina
32 Panama
40 Avocado
10 Tanner
11 Shilling
19 Newmarket
14 Mondeo
30 April
45 St Ives
22 Norwich
1 Bridgewater
15 Henry
48 Zebra
26 November
25 Gazelle
44 Penny
7 Scorpio
33 George
18 Corinth
2 Apricot

1 What was the writer George Orwell's real surname?

2 Which model of car built by Ford shares its name with an Italian island near Naples?

3 According to the nursery rhyme, where was I going to when 'I met a man with seven wives'?

4 Which world famous canal was opened in 1869?

5 What word is missing from the title of the Jeffrey Archer book, 'Not a ... more, not a ... less'?

6 Which English king, with the regnal number III, was the last to die in battle in 1485?

7 Which four-legged African animal is most associated with a type of pedestrian crossing?

8 What did the 'F' stand for in the name of the US president John F Kennedy?

9 New York City is sometimes referred to as 'The Big ...'?

10 Complete the title of the Carole King song, 'It Might As Well Rain Until ...'?

HOW TO PLAY AND SCORING

The answers to the questions are in the Wonderwall below. Write the number of your answer in the space provided, crossing answers off the Wall as you go. The time limit is 3 minutes. One point for each correct answer.

3 December
43 Ipswich
20 Blair
42 Wilson
49 Florin
21 Springbok
12 Fiesta
46 Francis
36 Major
35 Thetford
27 Richard
23 October
24 Pound
8 William
38 Suez
37 Fredericks
17 Aubergine
16 Kiel
31 Thatcher
41 Fitzgerald
47 Callaghan
6 Apple
4 Edward
39 Wildebeest
9 Fitzsimmons

11 ( ) The actor who played 'Jaws' in two James Bond films is Richard ...?

12 ( ) Prior to Lennox Lewis, the last world heavyweight boxing champion born in England was Bob ...?

13 ( ) Which British prime minister was born in Grantham in 1925?

14 ( ) In which month is Remembrance Sunday commemorated in the UK?

15 ( ) Which town is the home of the Jockey Club and Tattersalls?

16 ( ) What general name is given to a religious festival in Spanish-speaking countries?

17 ( ) Which male name was used by one of the girls in Enid Blyton's 'Famous Five' books?

18 ( ) What was the surname of Elsie, played by Pat Phoenix in 'Coronation Street'?

19 ( ) By what name is the alligator pear also known?

20 ( ) What is an alternative name for the gnu?

4 Memory Wonderwall

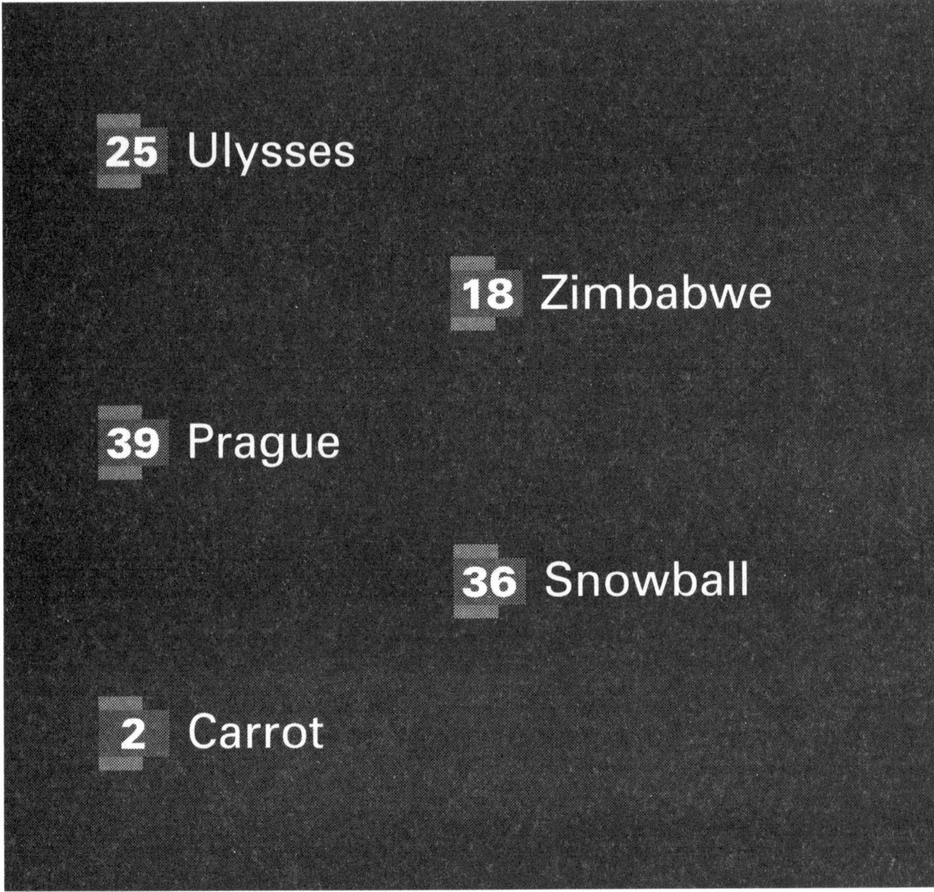

HOW TO PLAY

You have one minute to memorise the mini Wonderwall! Memorise both the word answer and its corresponding number. Then turn the page to answer the ten questions from memory.

FOR EXAMPLE

Question: What is the capital of Iceland?

Answer: 11. Reykjavik (*Scores 2 points*)

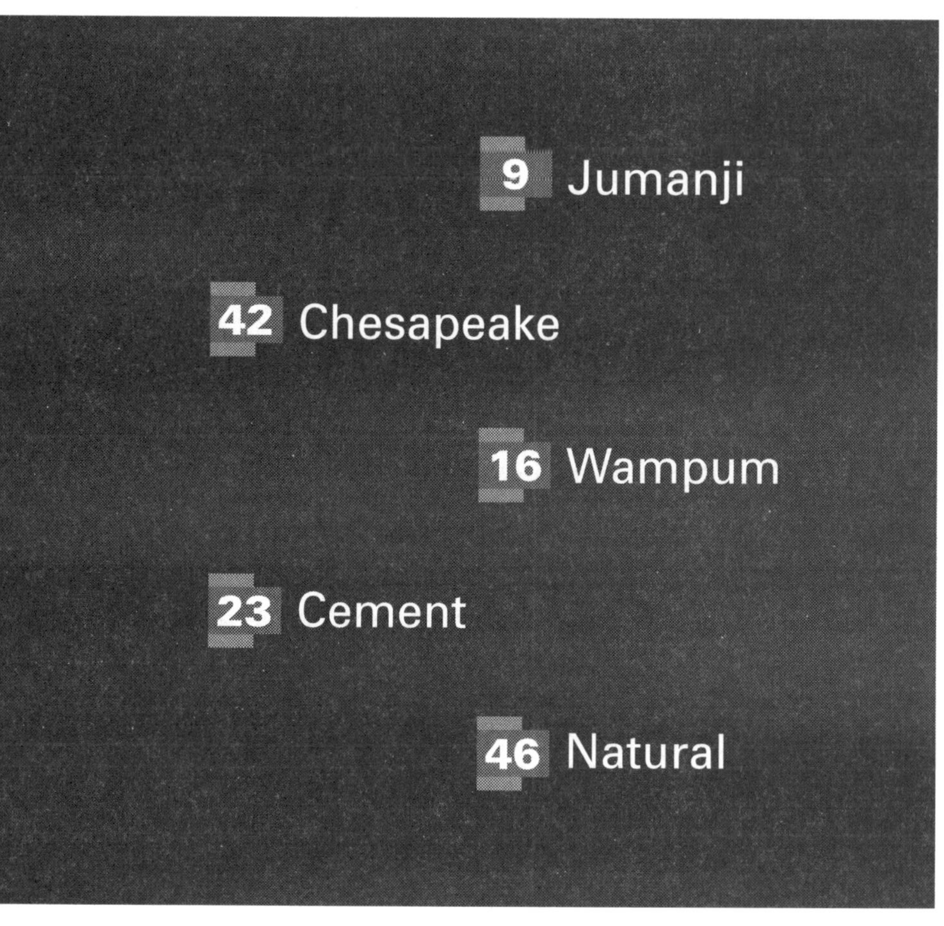

SCORING

Award yourself one point for answering the question correctly, and a bonus point for remembering the number that corresponds to your answer.

Turn page for questions

Round 4: Memory Wonderwall Questions

1. What is the name of the Simpson's pet cat in the cartoon series of the same name?

2. What were the strings of beads or shells called that were used as money by Native Americans?

3. Which breed of retriever gets its name from an inlet of the Atlantic Ocean between Maryland and Virginia?

4. Robin Williams played Alan Parrish in which 1995 film?

5. Molly and Leopold Bloom appear in which James Joyce novel?

6. A dish described as 'à la Crécy' contains which vegetable?

7. In which country was the cricketer Graeme Hick born?

8. In musical notation, which sign changes a sharp or flat note back to its original value?

9. Joseph Aspdin is best remembered for the invention of what?

10. Wenceslas Square is the main square of which European capital city?

Scorecard

Answers for Game Five are on page 157.

ROUND 1: THE WINNING LINE

Number of correct answers ---------

Add 2 points for creating the Winning Line ---------

(Maximum Score = 8) **Your Score**

ROUND 2: LOOKING AFTER NUMBER ONE
(Your score will be either 0 or 10) **Your Score**

ROUND 3: WONDERWALL
(Maximum Score = 20) **Your Score**

ROUND 4: MEMORY WONDERWALL
(Maximum Score = 20) **Your Score**

TOTAL SCORE

HOLIDAY SCORE

Go to the Holiday Prize Table on page 5 to find out whether your total score will take you around the world!

GAME SIX

Answers for Game Six on page 157. Scorecard page 65.

1 The Winning Line

HOW TO PLAY

First answer the following six questions in the spaces provided (Tip! Answers will be a number). Transfer your answers to the oval spaces in the Winning Line. If these answers add up to the winning number, you have a Winning Line! There is no time limit for this round.

1 If Gene Pitney was only a third of the time from Tulsa as his song title says, how many hours away would he be?

2 If Cornwall bordered 4 more counties, how many would it border in total?

3 If a silver wedding were to be celebrated eleven years earlier, after how many years would it be celebrated?

4 If a set of soccer goalposts were twice as high as normal, how many feet high would they be?

5 If there had been two more English Kings named William, what number would the next one be?

6 If Jeff Tracy had one less son in 'Thunderbirds', how many would he have?

Create your Winning Line:

+ + + + +

= Winning Number = 54

SCORING

Score one point for each question answered correctly, plus an additional two points if your answers successfully add up to the Winning Number.

2 Looking After Number One

HOW TO PLAY

Look at the following ten questions. Tick only those questions whose answers correspond with the winning number shown in the oval below the questions. There is no time limit for this round.

For example, if the Winning Number = 7

How many dwarfs lived with Snow White?

1 According to Meat Loaf, how many 'out of three ain't bad'?

2 How many balls make up the traditional sign of the pawnbroker?

3 Prince William, the eldest son of Prince Charles, was born in 198...?

4 The road also known as the 'Great North Road' is the 'A...'?

5 If you were slightly drunk, you might be described as having had how many 'over the eight'?

6 How many arms does a cricket umpire raise to indicate a bye?

7 According to the proverb, how many swallows do not 'make a summer'?

8 How many feet did Richard Wilson's character have in the grave, according to the title of the TV sitcom?

9 Complete the title of this A A Milne book, 'Now we are...'?

10 How many minutes is the 'warning' given for an impending nuclear attack?

WINNING NUMBER =

SCORING

Score ten points if your answers match exactly with those in the back of the book.

3 Wonderwall

13 BBC		34 Duck		28 Norway
	5 CIA		29 Apple	
32 Rome		40 Horseradish		
	10 Denmark		11 Cuckoo	
19 Saturn		14 Bottom		30 Snug
	45 Banger		22 Orange	
1 Milan		15 Taurus		48 Oberon
	26 Ireland		25 Iceland	
44 Mars		7 Paris		33 Sweden
	18 Stork		2 Scotland	

1 What is the 'B' in a BLT sandwich?

2 Which TV comedy series of the early 90s starred Ade Edmondson and Rik Mayall?

3 Which city is the permanent home of the Mona Lisa?

4 The motto of which organisation is 'Who Dares Wins'?

5 Which planet is not included in Holst's 'Planets Suite' because it had not been discovered when the piece was composed?

6 Which sauce has become the traditional British accompaniment to roast beef?

7 The national flag of which Scandinavian country has an offset yellow cross on a blue background?

8 Which part of the British Isles was known to the Romans as Hibernia?

9 According to folklore, which bird is said to bring newly-born children to their mothers?

10 Which 'Tropic' lies approximately 23½ degrees south of the Equator?

HOW TO PLAY AND SCORING

The answers to the questions are in the Wonderwall below. Write the number of your answer in the space provided, crossing answers off the Wall as you go. The time limit is 3 minutes. One point for each correct answer.

3 Mint
43 Banana
20 Anglesey
42 Crane
49 SAS
21 NASA
12 Finland
46 Iago
36 Wales
35 Cancer
27 Jupiter
23 Amsterdam
24 Neptune
8 Madrid
38 Butter
37 Bread
17 Redcurrant
16 MI5
31 Aries
41 Petruchio
47 Pluto
6 Bacon
4 Lindisfarne
39 Goose
9 Capricorn

11 ◯ Until superseded by the Euro, the Markka was the main unit of currency of which country?

12 ◯ George Bush Snr, the former president of the USA, was the director of which organization between 1976-81?

13 ◯ What name is given to a place where coins are made?

14 ◯ What can be a slang term for an old car or an ingredient of the dish 'toad in the hole'?

15 ◯ Which sign of the zodiac spans the months of April and May?

16 ◯ What goes after 'Real' and 'Atletico' to form the names of two famous football clubs?

17 ◯ Who is the King of the Fairies in Shakespeare's 'A Midsummer Night's Dream'?

18 ◯ In cricket, which bird is associated with being out without scoring any runs?

19 ◯ Who was the chief god of Roman mythology, associated with the Greek god Zeus?

20 ◯ Who had UK hits with 'Meet Me On The Corner' and 'Fog On The Tyne'?

4 Memory Wonderwall

HOW TO PLAY

You have one minute to memorise the mini Wonderwall! Memorise both the word answer and its corresponding number. Then turn the page to answer the ten questions from memory.

FOR EXAMPLE

Question: What is the capital of Iceland?
Answer: 11. Reykjavik (*Scores 2 points*)

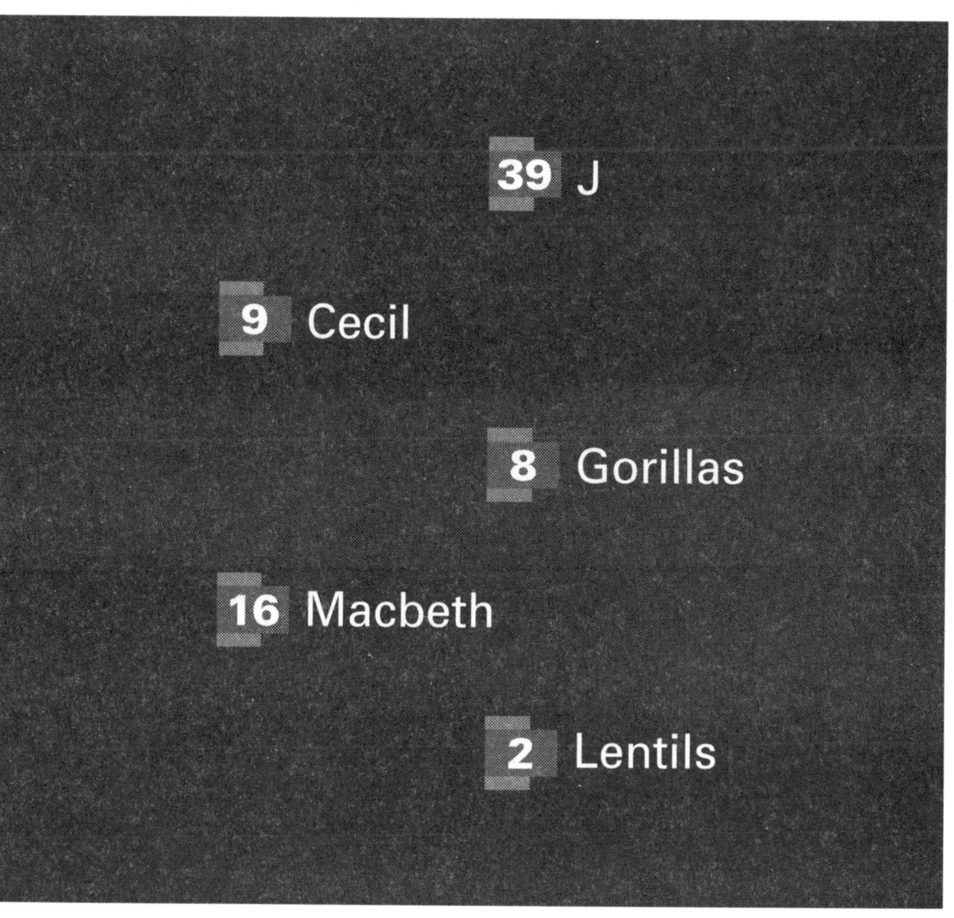

SCORING

Award yourself one point for answering the question correctly, and a bonus point for remembering the number that corresponds to your answer.

Turn page for questions

Round 4: Memory Wonderwall Questions

1 What was the first name of the poet C Day Lewis?

2 Io, Europa and Ganymede are three moons of which planet?

3 In classic French cookery, 'Conti' is the name given to dressings made from what?

4 By what nickname is the veteran DJ Alan Freeman known?

5 Dian Fossey is best known for her work with which animals?

6 Karl Marx's tomb is a landmark in which London cemetery?

7 What was Will Smith's letter designation after joining the 'Men in Black'?

8 Which Scottish king had a wife named Gruoch?

9 On which golf course did Nick Faldo win his first Open Championship?

10 Who wrote the chart-topping 'Nothing Compares 2 U' for Sinead O'Connor?

Scorecard

Answers for Game Six are on page 157.

ROUND 1: THE WINNING LINE

Number of correct answers ---------

Add 2 points for creating the Winning Line ---------

(Maximum Score = 8) **Your Score**

ROUND 2: LOOKING AFTER NUMBER ONE
(Your score will be either 0 or 10) **Your Score**

ROUND 3: WONDERWALL
(Maximum Score = 20) **Your Score**

ROUND 4: MEMORY WONDERWALL
(Maximum Score = 20) **Your Score**

TOTAL SCORE

HOLIDAY SCORE

Go to the Holiday Prize Table on page 5 to find out whether your total score will take you around the world!

GAME SEVEN

Answers for Game Seven on page 157. Scorecard page 75.

1 The Winning Line

HOW TO PLAY

First answer the following six questions in the spaces provided (Tip! Answers will be a number). Transfer your answers to the oval spaces in the Winning Line. If these answers add up to the winning number, you have a Winning Line! There is no time limit for this round.

1. If Henry VIII had been married twice as many times, how many wives would he have had?

2. If a cricket team had six more players on the field, how many would it have?

3. If the number of the motorway encircling London were twelve less, what would it be?

4 If it is 12 noon and you put your watch back nine hours, what 'o'clock' would it read?

5 If you took two dozen from three baker's dozens, how many would you have?

6 How many times could you fill a 400ml glass from a 2-litre bottle of water?

Create your Winning Line:

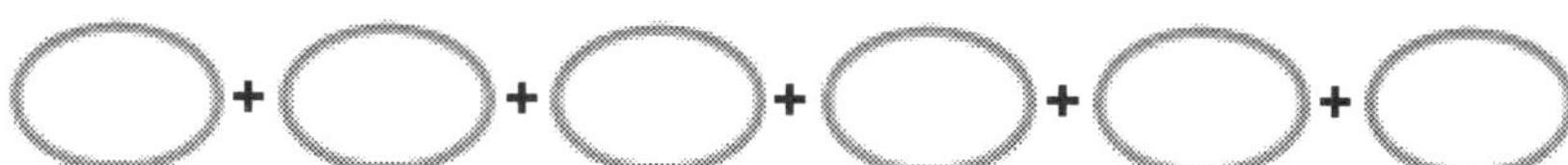

= Winning Number = 65

SCORING

Score one point for each question answered correctly, plus an additional two points if your answers successfully add up to the Winning Number.

2 Looking After Number One

HOW TO PLAY

Look at the following ten questions. Tick only those questions whose answers correspond with the winning number shown in the oval below the questions. There is no time limit for this round.

For example, if the Winning Number = 7

How many dwarfs lived with Snow White?

1 How many stars form the Plough, part of the Great Bear constellation?

2 Enid Blyton wrote a series of books about the Secret ...?

3 How many symmetrical segments does a snowflake have?

4 A bed with a canopy supported by a post at each corner is sometimes referred to as a '... poster bed'?

5 What is the minimum number of games needed to win a set in tennis?

6 According to the proverb, 'a stitch in time saves' – how many?

7 How many days did the war between Israel and its Arab neighbours last in 1967?

8 How many senses does a normal human being have?

9 How many 'Friends' are there in the American TV series of the same name?

10 How many musicians comprise a septet?

WINNING NUMBER = 

SCORING

Score ten points if your answers match exactly with those in the back of the book.

3 Wonderwall

13 Jack
34 Pantry
28 Devon
5 Pearl
29 Blinked
32 Joey
40 Porcupine
10 Hall
11 Friday
19 Sneezed
14 Dublin
30 Cardiff
45 Willie
22 Horse
1 Kent
15 Bakerloo
48 Cried
26 Diamond
25 Ruby
44 Thursday
7 Tuesday
33 Sunday
18 Edinburgh
2 Porpoise

1 Where is the Dewey decimal classification system most likely to be used?

2 What name is given to a baby kangaroo?

3 The name of which precious stone is sometimes used in rhyming slang for a curry?

4 The Millennium Stadium is in which capital city of the British Isles?

5 The name of which playing card is the same as the name of a device for lifting cars?

6 If somebody says 'gesundheit' to you, what are you most likely to have done?

7 In which county is Chatsworth House, the home of the Duke of Devonshire?

8 The traditional day for eating pancakes is Shrove ...?

9 Which animal might be described as porcine?

10 Which London Underground line has no terminal stations?

HOW TO PLAY AND SCORING

The answers to the questions are in the Wonderwall below. Write the number of your answer in the space provided, crossing answers off the Wall as you go. The time limit is 3 minutes. One point for each correct answer.

3 Metropolitan	43 Deuce	20 Lancashire
42 Pig	49 Emerald	
21 Cheshire	12 Derbyshire	46 London
36 Northern	35 Coughed	
27 Queen	23 Belfast	24 Billie
8 Jimmy	38 Circle	
37 Library	17 Armadillo	16 Kitchen
31 Bathroom	41 Monday	
47 Victoria	6 Hiccuped	4 Sapphire
39 Ace	9 Johnny	

11 ( ) In which room of the house is a bidet most likely to be found?

12 ( ) Complete the title of the US TV series set in Cicely, Alaska, '...Exposure'?

13 ( ) What is the name of the groundkeeper at Bart Simpson's school in the TV series 'The Simpsons'?

14 ( ) Which animal has defensive quills or spines on its body and tail?

15 ( ) What might a person have done if an involuntary spasm of the diaphragm is linked with a sudden closure of the glottis?

16 ( ) With which rock group was Brian May the lead guitarist?

17 ( ) The actress who became best known as Raquel Wolstenhulme in 'Coronation Street' is Sarah ...?

18 ( ) The WWII British cruiser moored on the river Thames is HMS ...?

19 ( ) Since 1931, on which day of the week have General Elections been held in the UK?

20 ( ) In which kind of city did the Wizard of Oz live?

4 Memory Wonderwall

43 Lewes

22 Heart

48 China

34 Toothpaste

21 Platypus

HOW TO PLAY

You have one minute to memorise the mini Wonderwall! Memorise both the word answer and its corresponding number. Then turn the page to answer the ten questions from memory.

FOR EXAMPLE

Question: What is the capital of Iceland?

Answer: 11. Reykjavik (*Scores 2 points*)

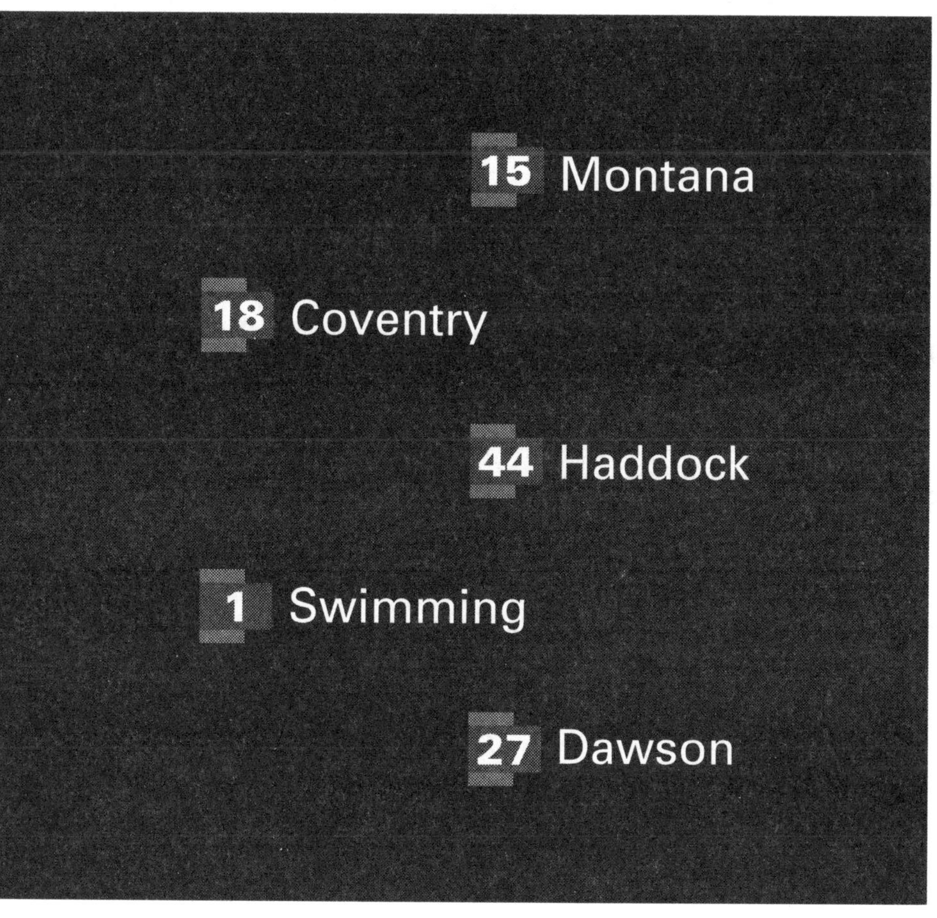

SCORING

Award yourself one point for answering the question correctly, and a bonus point for remembering the number that corresponds to your answer.

Turn page for questions

Round 4: Memory Wonderwall Questions

1. Benjamin Britten's 'War Requiem' was first performed in the cathedral of which city?

2. What was the first commodity to be advertised on British TV?

3. In which sport did the American Matt Biondi win five Olympic gold medals?

4. What was the surname of Jack, Leonardo DiCaprio's character in the film 'Titanic'?

5. At which battle of 1264 did Simon de Montfort defeat the forces of Henry III?

6. In which organ of the human body are there two ventricles and two atria?

7. Which country was the main setting for the best seller 'Wild Swans'?

8. In which US state is the Little Bighorn National Monument?

9. Which fish is traditionally used to make the Scottish soup cullen skink?

10. The name of which Australian mammal means 'flat-foot'?

Scorecard

Answers for Game Seven are on page 157.

ROUND 1: THE WINNING LINE

Number of correct answers ---------

Add 2 points for creating the Winning Line ---------

(Maximum Score = 8) **Your Score**

ROUND 2: LOOKING AFTER NUMBER ONE

(Your score will be either 0 or 10) **Your Score**

ROUND 3: WONDERWALL

(Maximum Score = 20) **Your Score**

ROUND 4: MEMORY WONDERWALL

(Maximum Score = 20) **Your Score**

TOTAL SCORE

HOLIDAY SCORE

Go to the Holiday Prize Table on page 5 to find out whether your total score will take you around the world!

GAME EIGHT

Answers for Game Eight on page 158. Scorecard page 85.

1 The Winning Line

HOW TO PLAY

First answer the following six questions in the spaces provided (Tip! Answers will be a number). Transfer your answers to the oval spaces in the Winning Line. If these answers add up to the winning number, you have a Winning Line! There is no time limit for this round.

1 If Jake the Peg rode the Aintree Grand National winner, how many legs would they have between them?

2 If you divide what you receive for passing 'GO' in 'Monopoly' by an outer bulls-eye on a dartboard, what are you left with?

3 If you bought beer at £2 a pint, how much would 1½ gallons cost you?

4 If the floodlights fail two-thirds of the way through the first half of a football match, how many minutes will have been played?

5 If you subtract the number of stripes for an Army corporal from that of a sergeant, how many do you have left?

6 Add together the number of US states that either begin with the words 'South' or 'West': how many do you have?

Create your Winning Line:

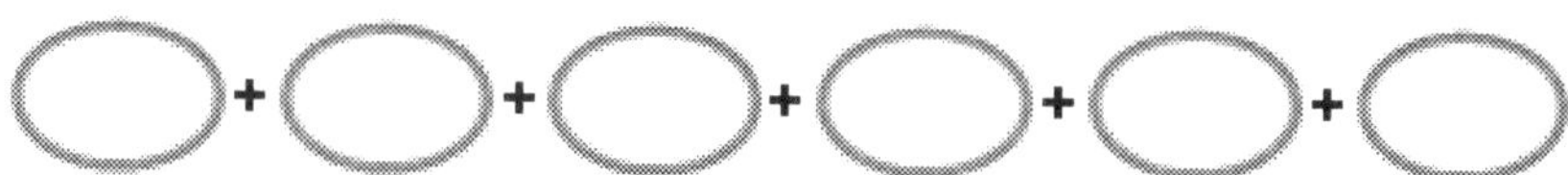

= Winning Number = 73

SCORING

Score one point for each question answered correctly, plus an additional two points if your answers successfully add up to the Winning Number.

2 Looking After Number One

HOW TO PLAY

Look at the following ten questions. Tick only those questions whose answers correspond with the winning number shown in the oval below the questions. There is no time limit for this round.

For example, if the Winning Number = 7

How many dwarfs lived with Snow White? 

1 On what date in February does St Valentine's Day fall? 

2 How many oarsmen take part in the University Boat Race? 

3 How many weeks did Bryan Adams spend at the top of the UK singles charts with '(Everything I Do) I Do It For You'? 

4 In imperial weights, how many ounces are equal to one pound? 

5 According to the Bible, how many attended the Last Supper? 

6 What is 2 multiplied to the power of 4?

7 What number is known in French as quinze?

8 What is the minimum age at which a person can legally buy a ticket for the National Lottery?

9 As of April 2002, how many member countries comprise the European Union?

10 What number shirt does the full back in a rugby union team usually wear?

WINNING NUMBER = 

SCORING

Score ten points if your answers match exactly with those in the back of the book.

3 Wonderwall

13 Vietnam	34 Green	28 Blackwood
5 Japan	29 French	
32 Rabbit	40 German	
10 Balance	11 Iodine	
19 Institution	14 Sheep	30 Brazil
45 Danish	22 Hearing	
1 Yellow	15 Marlborough	48 Wellington
26 Blue	25 Swedish	
44 Internal	7 Mustard	33 Hold
18 Hair	2 Voice	

1. Which country's national flag features a solid red circle on a white background?
2. One of the suspects in the board game 'Cluedo' is Colonel ...?
3. In 1814, Arthur Wellesley became the first Duke of ...?
4. What do the Americans call what we call the bonnet on a car?
5. Who or what was Brian in the TV animation 'The Magic Roundabout'?
6. From which European language does Afrikaans originate?
7. What do you often lose if you suffer from laryngitis?
8. What is the predominant colour of the first choice shirts worn by Chelsea FC?
9. What does the 'I' stand for in the abbreviation RNLI?
10. What is the official country residence of the British Prime Minister?

HOW TO PLAY AND SCORING

The answers to the questions are in the Wonderwall below. Write the number of your answer in the space provided, crossing answers off the Wall as you go. The time limit is 3 minutes. One point for each correct answer.

3 Dog
43 Vinegar
20 Salt
42 White
49 Westminster
21 Cow
12 Chequers
46 Hood
36 Pakistan
35 International
27 Iron
23 Pepper
24 Edinburgh
8 Caboose
38 Sight
37 Checkers
17 Indonesia
16 Snail
31 Trunk
41 Red
47 Whitehouse
6 Norfolk
4 Curry
39 Fender
9 Dutch

11 What kind of animal could be a Friesian, Jersey or Aberdeen Angus?

12 Who is Jennifer Saunder's regular comedy partner?

13 What name is given to the act of listening to evidence in a court of law, especially by a judge with no jury?

14 According to the song, what did Nellie the Elephant pack when she 'said goodbye to the circus'?

15 In which British city are the Royal Mile and Arthur's Seat?

16 Mick Hucknall is the lead singer with Simply ...?

17 Which chemical element has the symbol I?

18 In the home, how is a dilute solution of acetic acid more commonly known?

19 Of which country was Benazir Bhutto the first female prime minister?

20 What is an alternative name for the board game draughts?

4 Memory Wonderwall

HOW TO PLAY

You have one minute to memorise the mini Wonderwall! Memorise both the word answer and its corresponding number. Then turn the page to answer the ten questions from memory.

FOR EXAMPLE

Question: What is the capital of Iceland?

Answer: 11. Reykjavik *(Scores 2 points)*

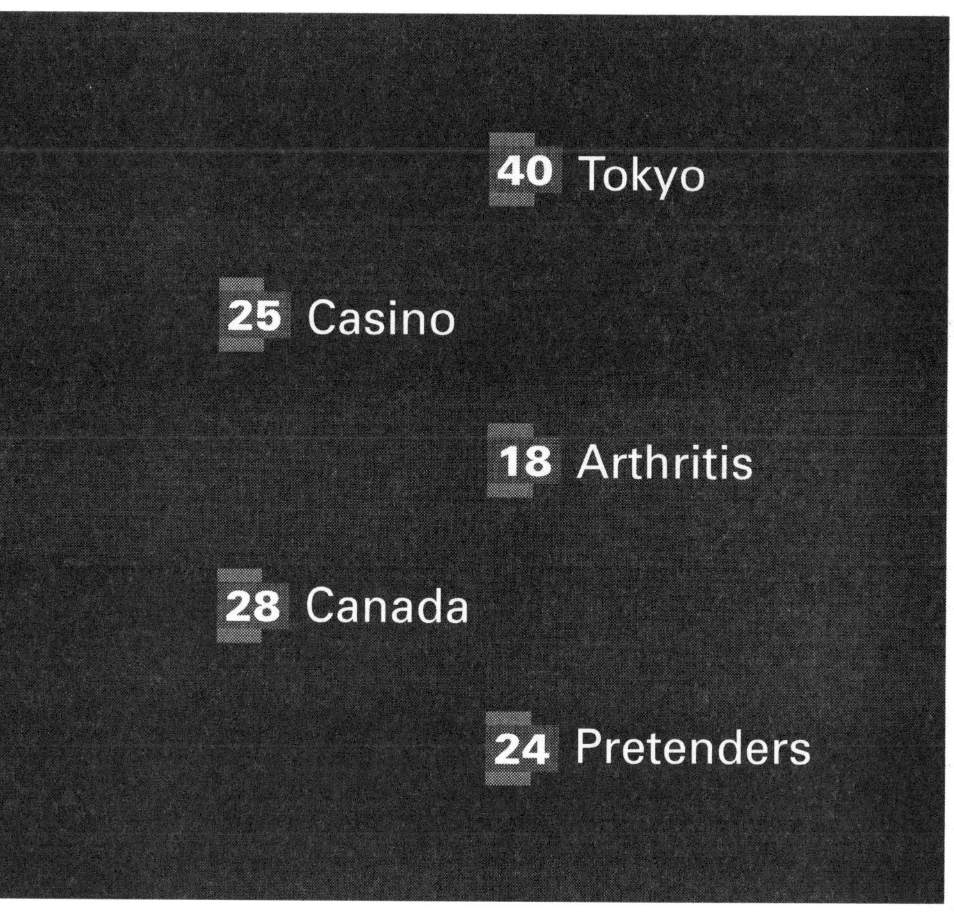

SCORING

Award yourself one point for answering the question correctly, and a bonus point for remembering the number that corresponds to your answer.

Turn page for questions

Round 4: Memory Wonderwall Questions

1. Which 1995 film starred Robert De Niro, Sharon Stone and Joe Pesci?

2. Which poet was a librarian at Hull University?

3. Rheumatoid, osteo and septic are the three main types of which ailment?

4. What is a penguins' breeding ground called?

5. Chrissie Hynde is the lead singer with which group?

6. Which city was originally due to host the cancelled 1940 Summer Olympic Games?

7. If a dish is described as 'à la Florentine', with which vegetable has it been prepared?

8. What was the name of the frog that featured in 'Hector's House'?

9. In which county is Alton Towers amusement park?

10. In which modern day country did the Klondike Gold Rush take place?

Scorecard

Answers for Game Eight are on page 158.

ROUND 1: THE WINNING LINE

Number of correct answers ---------

Add 2 points for creating the Winning Line ---------

(Maximum Score = 8) **Your Score**

ROUND 2: LOOKING AFTER NUMBER ONE
(Your score will be either 0 or 10) **Your Score**

ROUND 3: WONDERWALL
(Maximum Score = 20) **Your Score**

ROUND 4: MEMORY WONDERWALL
(Maximum Score = 20) **Your Score**

TOTAL SCORE

HOLIDAY SCORE

Go to the Holiday Prize Table on page 5 to find out whether your total score will take you around the world!

GAME NINE

Answers for Game Nine on page 158. Scorecard page 95.

1 The Winning Line

HOW TO PLAY

First answer the following six questions in the spaces provided (Tip! Answers will be a number). Transfer your answers to the oval spaces in the Winning Line. If these answers add up to the winning number, you have a Winning Line! There is no time limit for this round.

1. If Judas Iscariot received only one tenth as much silver as the Bible relates, how many pieces would he have got?

2. If a person has been eligible to vote in a UK General Election for the past nine years, how old are they?

3. If you lost half of the black playing cards from a standard pack, how many cards would you be left with?

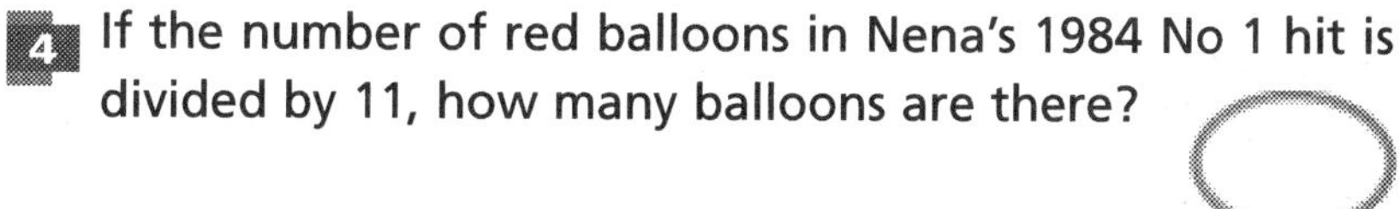

4 If the number of red balloons in Nena's 1984 No 1 hit is divided by 11, how many balloons are there?

5 How many legs would Enid Blyton's 'Famous Five' have if the two girls left?

6 If a person only has a quarter of the number of 'winks' in a short nap, how many have they taken?

Create your Winning Line:

◯ + ◯ + ◯ + ◯ + ◯ + ◯

= Winning Number = 96

SCORING

Score one point for each question answered correctly, plus an additional two points if your answers successfully add up to the Winning Number.

2 Looking After Number One

HOW TO PLAY

Look at the following ten questions. Tick only those questions whose answers correspond with the winning number shown in the oval below the questions. There is no time limit for this round.

For example, if the Winning Number = 7

How many dwarfs lived with Snow White?

1 The title of the 1984 sequel film to '2001: A Space Odyssey' is '20...'?

2 A dodecagon is a geometric figure with how many sides?

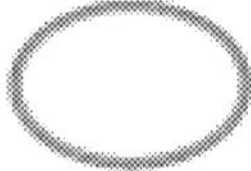

3 According to Andy Warhol, everyone will be world famous for how many minutes?

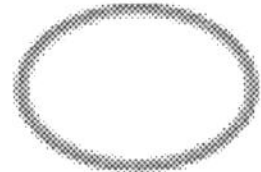

4 Unless it falls on a Sunday, on what day in August does the grouse shooting season start in Britain?

5 How many points is a starter question worth on 'University Challenge'?

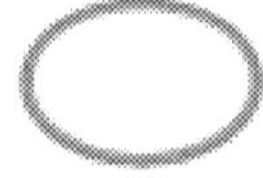

6 Which King Louis of France was known as the 'Sun King'?

7 The Battle of Waterloo took place in 18...?

8 How many 'guns' are fired in a basic Royal Salute?

9 According to the proverb, possession is how many points of the law?

10 In 1888, how many founder members of the English Football League were there?

WINNING NUMBER =

SCORING

Score ten points if your answers match exactly with those in the back of the book.

3 Wonderwall

13 Bear
34 Warsaw
28 Comma
5 Rome
29 Mongoose
32 Spain
40 Polo
10 Italy
11 Python
19 Resolution
14 Golf
30 Violin
45 Aquarius
22 Leo
1 Apostrophe
15 France
48 Rugby
26 Greece
25 Sternum
44 Panther
7 Cello
33 Reservation
18 Foot
2 Inch

1. The peseta was the main unit of currency of which country?
2. What is the anatomical name for the the human kneecap?
3. What is a Scottish name for a small island or small area of high land?
4. Who or what was Bagheera in the 'Jungle Book' stories by Rudyard Kipling?
5. What is an alternative name for a pledge or promise made on New Year's Eve?
6. Which Panamanian city stands at the Caribbean end of the Panama Canal?
7. According to the proverb, all roads lead to which city?
8. In which sport might a 'nightwatchman' be employed?
9. If your birthday falls on St Valentine's Day, under which sign of the zodiac were you born?
10. Which instrument is played by the leader of a modern symphony orchestra?

HOW TO PLAY AND SCORING

The answers to the questions are in the Wonderwall below. Write the number of your answer in the space provided, crossing answers off the Wall as you go. The time limit is 3 minutes. One point for each correct answer.

3 Bracket
43 Oboe
20 Paris
42 Portugal
49 Furlong
21 Jerusalem
12 Colon
46 Scapula
36 Berlin
35 Resignation
27 Piano
23 Mile
24 Badminton
8 Period
38 Gemini
37 Aries
17 Revolution
16 Yard
31 Revelation
41 Clavicle
47 Cricket
6 Virgo
4 Radius
39 Wolf
9 Patella

11 What unit of imperial measurement takes its name from the Latin for 'thousand'?

12 What is the name of the country home of the Duke of Beaufort?

13 What kind of action brought Napoleon, Lenin and Castro to power?

14 Which country is separated from Sicily by the Strait of Messina?

15 Complete the name of the comedy duo, 'Hinge and ...'?

16 On a musical score, which word means 'soft'?

17 A broken arm might be set in plaster of ...?

18 Which animal might be black, brown, polar or grizzly?

19 What is the surname of the co-presenter and referee of 'Big Break' with Jim Davidson?

20 What is half of the diameter of a circle known as?

4 Memory Wonderwall

18 Hovis

12 Danegeld

2 Billy Bunter

25 Elk

24 Metronome

HOW TO PLAY

You have one minute to memorise the mini Wonderwall! Memorise both the word answer and its corresponding number. Then turn the page to answer the ten questions from memory.

FOR EXAMPLE

Question: What is the capital of Iceland?
Answer: 11. Reykjavik (*Scores 2 points*)

SCORING

Award yourself one point for answering the question correctly, and a bonus point for remembering the number that corresponds to your answer.

Turn page for questions

Round 4: Memory Wonderwall Questions

1 Which tax was paid by the Saxons in England to buy peace from the Danish invaders?

2 The sackbut was an early form of which musical instrument?

3 Which area of Spain has a name meaning 'savage coast'?

4 Besides Lingfield Park and Southwell, which other British horse racing course has an all-weather track?

5 What is the European name for what North Americans call a moose?

6 Which schoolboy is known as the 'Fat Owl of the Remove'?

7 Which proprietary brand name is taken from the Latin meaning 'strength of man'?

8 What is the vocation of Susan Sarandon's character in 'Dead Man Walking'?

9 What aid to musicians was invented by the German Johann Maelzel in 1816?

10 What must you not employ when speaking on the radio programme 'Just A Minute'?

Scorecard

Answers for Game Nine are on page 158.

ROUND 1: THE WINNING LINE

Number of correct answers ---------

Add 2 points for creating the Winning Line ---------

(Maximum Score = 8) **Your Score**

ROUND 2: LOOKING AFTER NUMBER ONE
(Your score will be either 0 or 10) **Your Score**

ROUND 3: WONDERWALL
(Maximum Score = 20) **Your Score**

ROUND 4: MEMORY WONDERWALL
(Maximum Score = 20) **Your Score**

TOTAL SCORE

HOLIDAY SCORE

Go to the Holiday Prize Table on page 5 to find out whether your total score will take you around the world!

GAME TEN

Answers for Game Ten on page 158. Scorecard page 105.

1 The Winning Line

HOW TO PLAY

First answer the following six questions in the spaces provided (Tip! Answers will be a number). Transfer your answers to the oval spaces in the Winning Line. If these answers add up to the winning number, you have a Winning Line! There is no time limit for this round.

1 If one-third of the consonants were removed from our alphabet, how many letters would be left?

2 Divide the 'Haircut' pop group by the number of cubic centimetres in the name of the group who sang 'Rubber Bullets': what have you got?

3 What is the answer if you divide the number of seconds in a minute, by the number of minutes in an hour?

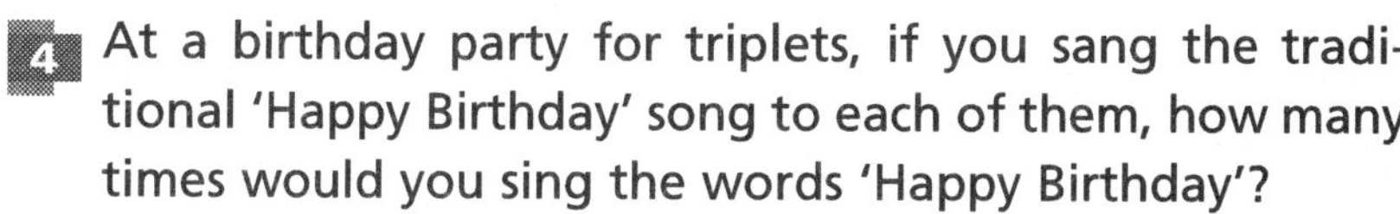

4 At a birthday party for triplets, if you sang the traditional 'Happy Birthday' song to each of them, how many times would you sing the words 'Happy Birthday'?

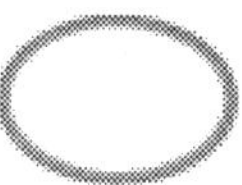

5 If you have a third of a group of sextuplets and half a group of quadruplets, how many people do you have altogether?

6 How many years of bad luck can you expect if you break three mirrors?

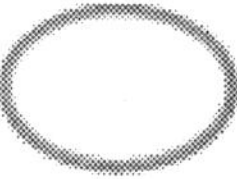

Create your Winning Line:

○ + ○ + ○ + ○ + ○ + ○

= Winning Number = 67

SCORING

Score one point for each question answered correctly, plus an additional two points if your answers successfully add up to the Winning Number.

Looking After Number One

HOW TO PLAY

Look at the following ten questions. Tick only those questions whose answers correspond with the winning number shown in the oval below the questions. There is no time limit for this round.

For example, if the Winning Number = 7

How many dwarfs lived with Snow White?

1 In the rhyme about Lizzie Borden, how many 'whacks with an axe' did she give her mother?

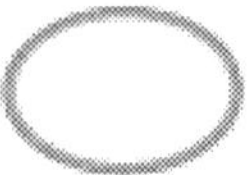

2 According to the proverb, at what age does life begin?

3 For how many days and nights did Jesus fast in the wilderness, according to the Bible?

4 Japan attacked Pearl Harbor in December 19...?

5 What is the youngest age at which a person can be called a quinquagenarian?

6 How many degrees are equal to half a right angle?

7 What is the number of the 'Street' in the musical by Al Dubin and Harry Warren?

8 According to Paul Simon's song, how many ways are there 'to leave your lover'?

9 What is the square root of the number on Pennsylvania Avenue of the White House in Washington DC?

10 What number goes before 'something' to give the title of a US TV series about angst-ridden Philadelphians in the 1980s and 90s?

WINNING NUMBER = 40

SCORING

Score ten points if your answers match exactly with those in the back of the book.

3 Wonderwall

13 Gluttony	34 Edward	28 Surgeon
5 Harold	29 Bombay	
32 Butcher	40 Bangalore	
10 Pulsars	11 Burnley	
19 Spaghetti	14 Delhi	30 Georgia
45 Comets	22 Meteors	
1 Sloth	15 Bradford	48 Brown
26 Brewer	25 Germany	
44 Canneloni	7 Jogger	33 John
18 William	2 Asteroids	

1 What type of pasta gives its name to a major road interchange just north of Birmingham?

2 What is the profession of someone described as an SRN?

3 Which English king was killed at the Battle of Hastings?

4 With which Indian city was Mother Teresa most associated?

5 What was the name of Bill Haley's backing group?

6 What did the 'B' stand for in the name of the US president, Lyndon B Johnson?

7 The front man with the Rolling Stones is Mick ...?

8 Which of the Seven Deadly Sins is also used to describe a social gathering of lions?

9 Which snooker player is nicknamed the 'Whirlwind'?

10 Which country is known as 'Deutschland' in its own language?

HOW TO PLAY AND SCORING

The answers to the questions are in the Wonderwall below. Write the number of your answer in the space provided, crossing answers off the Wall as you go. The time limit is 3 minutes. One point for each correct answer.

3 Lust
43 Satellites
20 Ravioli
42 Blue
49 New Mexico
21 Henry
12 Nurse
46 Bolton
36 Anger
35 Vermicelli
27 Blackpool
23 Greene
24 Pride
8 Jigger
38 Baines
37 Jumble
17 White
16 Baker
31 Jagger
41 Denmark
47 Calcutta
6 Madras
4 Macaroni
39 Crimson
9 Juggler

11 What is the first name of the mischievous schoolboy created by Richmal Crompton?

12 Which English football league club plays its home matches at Turf Moor?

13 Complete the line from the song 'Yankee Doodle', 'Stuck a feather in his cap and called it ...'?

14 By what alternative name are the minor planets of our solar system also known?

15 Complete the title of the John Osborne play, 'Look Back in ...'?

16 When dried and eaten, the bummalo fish is sometimes known as '... Duck'?

17 Which former state of the Soviet Union has the same name as a US state?

18 The head of the Cartwright family in 'Bonanza' was played by Lorne ...?

19 What surname is shared by two men who have portrayed Doctor Who on TV?

20 What is the general term for a person who can keep several objects in the air at one time?

Memory Wonderwall

2 Krajicek

5 Weather

28 Pregnant

30 Collector

9 Okapi

HOW TO PLAY

You have one minute to memorise the mini Wonderwall! Memorise both the word answer and its corresponding number. Then turn the page to answer the ten questions from memory.

FOR EXAMPLE

Question: What is the capital of Iceland?

Answer: 11. Reykjavik (*Scores 2 points)*

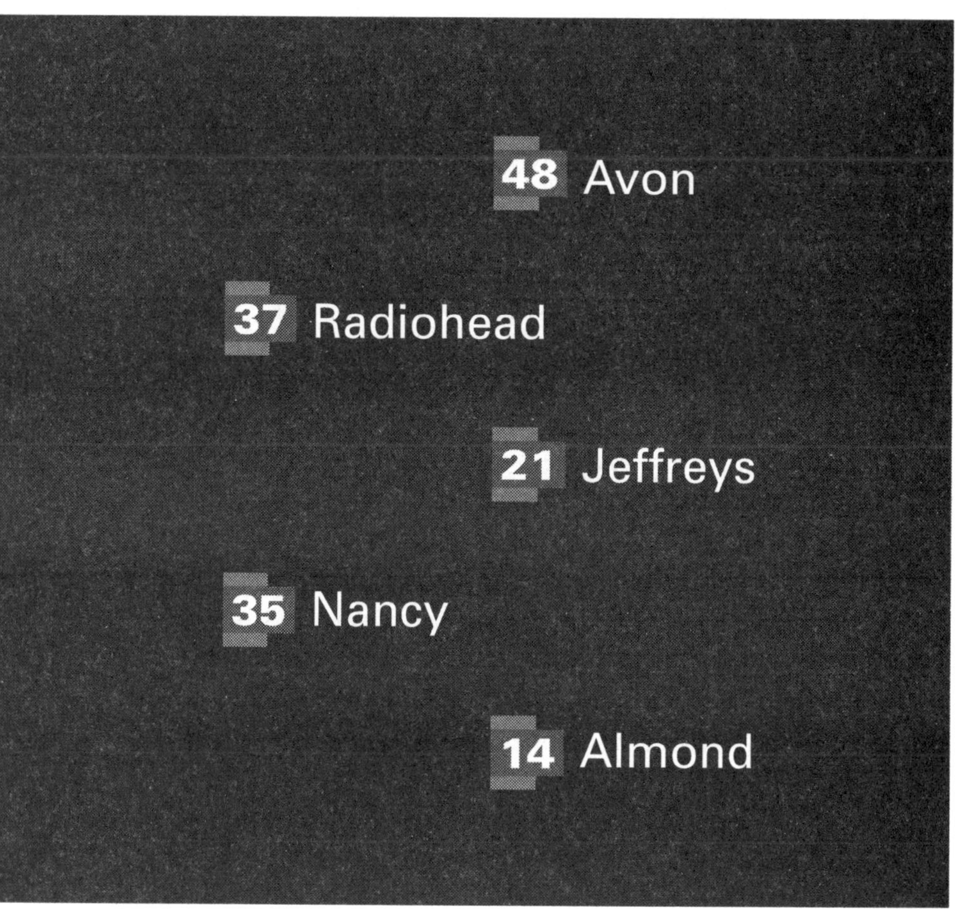

SCORING

Award yourself one point for answering the question correctly, and a bonus point for remembering the number that corresponds to your answer.

Turn page for questions

Round 4: Memory Wonderwall Questions

1 The Clifton Suspension Bridge spans which British river?

2 What does Arnold Schwarzenegger become in the film 'Junior'?

3 What sort of programme would Peter Cockcroft most probably present on TV?

4 Who was the notorious judge at the 'Bloody Assizes' of 1685?

5 Which band's first entry in the UK singles charts was 'Anyone Can Play Guitar' in 1993?

6 Which nut is the main flavouring of macaroon biscuits?

7 The three components of a basic semiconductor transistor are the base, emitter and which other?

8 Which relative of the giraffe was unknown outside Africa until 1901?

9 Which member of the Mitford family wrote 'Love in a Cold Climate'?

10 In 1996, who interrupted Pete Sampras's run of eight consecutive Wimbledon Men's Singles titles?

Scorecard

Answers for Game Ten are on page 158.

ROUND 1: THE WINNING LINE

Number of correct answers ---------

Add 2 points for creating the Winning Line ---------

(Maximum Score = 8) **Your Score**

ROUND 2: LOOKING AFTER NUMBER ONE
(Your score will be either 0 or 10) **Your Score**

ROUND 3: WONDERWALL
(Maximum Score = 20) **Your Score**

ROUND 4: MEMORY WONDERWALL
(Maximum Score = 20) **Your Score**

TOTAL SCORE

HOLIDAY SCORE

Go to the Holiday Prize Table on page 5 to find out whether your total score will take you around the world!

Game Eleven

Answers for Game Eleven on page 158. Scorecard page 115.

1 The Winning Line

HOW TO PLAY

First answer the following six questions in the spaces provided (Tip! Answers will be a number). Transfer your answers to the oval spaces in the Winning Line. If these answers add up to the winning number, you have a Winning Line! There is no time limit for this round.

1. If three pieces have been taken, how many pieces in total are still on a draughts board?

2. If there were one less football club in the English Premiership, how many would there be?

3. If the number of Martian moons is subtracted from the number of major planets in our solar system, what number is left?

4 What number do you get if you add together the four digits you dial for BT's 'Call Return' system?

5 If the cross of St Andrew were removed from the Union Flag, how many saint's crosses would be left?

6 What number do you get if you divide the value of the highest Bank of England banknote by the value of the lowest?

Create your Winning Line:

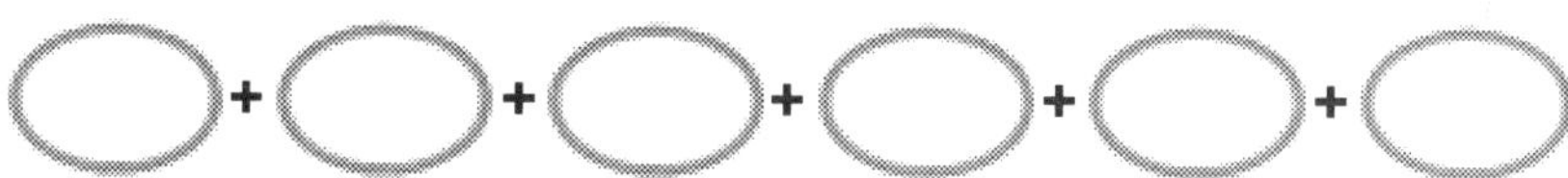

= Winning Number = 72

SCORING

Score one point for each question answered correctly, plus an additional two points if your answers successfully add up to the Winning Number.

2 Looking After Number One

HOW TO PLAY

Look at the following ten questions. Tick only those questions whose answers correspond with the winning number shown in the oval below the questions. There is no time limit for this round.

For example, if the Winning Number = 7

How many dwarfs lived with Snow White?

1 The great Californian Gold Rush began in 18...?

2 What number preceded 'Crash' to give Suzi Quatro a UK No 3 hit in 1973?

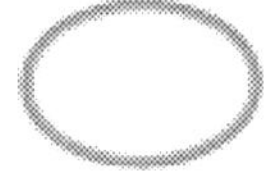

3 According to Douglas Adams, what is the answer to Life, the Universe and Everything?

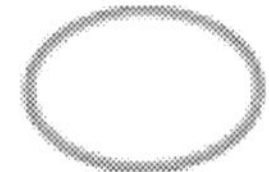

4 What number president of the USA is George W Bush?

5 What is the next number in this sequence, 1, 4, 9, 16, 25, 36 ...?

6 How many numbered balls are used in the UK national lottery draw?

7 On a compass, how many degrees are there between north and north-east?

8 When telephoning the UK from France or Germany, the code you should use is 00...?

9 How many states of the USA were there immediately prior to WWII?

10 If you are two years away from your golden wedding anniversary, how many years have you been married?

WINNING NUMBER =

SCORING

Score ten points if your answers match exactly with those in the back of the book.

3 Wonderwall

13 Goose
34 Sheffield
28 Pigeon
5 Amber
29 Hexagon
32 Heptagon
40 Heel
10 Leicester
11 Easy
19 Plain
14 Flank
30 Red
45 Octagon
22 Sting
1 Federal
15 Ignorant
48 Spring
26 Charlton
25 Brentford
44 Chilli
7 Wrist
33 Saffron
18 Ginger
2 Fulham

1 What shape is each individual cell in the honeycomb of a beehive?

2 Who was the lead singer with The Police?

3 What is the bottom colour on a normal set of traffic lights?

4 Which London football club shares its name with a type of 18th century porcelain?

5 According to the nursery rhyme, which adjective describes Simon, the boy who met a pie-man?

6 What meat do Americans traditionally eat on Thanksgiving Day?

7 To which part of the body is the Achilles tendon connected?

8 What is the first name of Julia Sawalha's character in the TV comedy 'Absolutely Fabulous'?

9 What does the 'F' stand for in the abbreviation FBI?

10 What do the Americans call what we call a bowler hat?

HOW TO PLAY AND SCORING

The answers to the questions are in the Wonderwall below. Write the number of your answer in the space provided, crossing answers off the Wall as you go. The time limit is 3 minutes. One point for each correct answer.

3 Simple
43 Derby
20 Cumin
42 Triangle
49 Basic
21 Lincoln
12 Knee
46 Chelsea
36 Prang
35 Arsenal
27 Force
23 Shoulder
24 Duck
8 Chicken
38 Jet
37 Stung
17 Finger
16 Pentagon
31 Prong
41 Turquoise
47 Turkey
6 Paprika
4 Green
39 Nottingham
9 Field

11 ◯ What is an RAF slang word for crashing an aircraft?

12 ◯ A person who is cowardly might be named after which bird?

13 ◯ Which city stands on the banks of the river Trent?

14 ◯ What kind of 'Lover' was a UK No 1 for Phil Collins and Philip Bailey in 1985?

15 ◯ By what name is the headquarters of the US Department of Defense more commonly known?

16 ◯ In heraldry, what name is given to the background of a shield?

17 ◯ What name is given to a collection of weapons?

18 ◯ The rock group Cream consisted of Eric Clapton, Jack Bruce and ... Baker?

19 ◯ What does a cricket umpire raise to indicate a batsman is out?

20 ◯ What is a hard semi-precious variety of lignite?

4 Memory Wonderwall

HOW TO PLAY

You have one minute to memorise the mini Wonderwall! Memorise both the word answer and its corresponding number. Then turn the page to answer the ten questions from memory.

FOR EXAMPLE

Question: What is the capital of Iceland?

Answer: 11. Reykjavik (*Scores 2 points)*

9 Macedonia

4 Cassiopeia

46 Netball

44 Philadelphia

16 Benvolio

SCORING

Award yourself one point for answering the question correctly, and a bonus point for remembering the number that corresponds to your answer.

Turn page for questions

Round 4: Memory Wonderwall Questions

1 What is the name of Montague's nephew in Shakespeare's 'Romeo and Juliet'?

2 Which shaggy horned variety of cattle is native to Tibet?

3 Alexander the Great was king of where?

4 From which country did Eritrea gain independence in 1993?

5 Which constellation is named after the wife of King Cepheus and the mother of Andromeda?

6 Billed as the most seen person on British TV, on what did Carol Hersey appear?

7 Which sport is played 7-a-side in 4 periods of 15 minutes?

8 Which Lerner and Loewe musical is set in a legendary Scottish village?

9 What turns a Virgin Mary into a Bloody Mary?

10 In which 1993 film did Denzel Washington play the lawyer Joe Miller, representing Andrew Beckett, played by Tom Hanks?

Scorecard

Answers for Game Eleven are on page 158.

ROUND 1: THE WINNING LINE

Number of correct answers ---------

Add 2 points for creating the Winning Line ---------

(Maximum Score = 8) **Your Score**

ROUND 2: LOOKING AFTER NUMBER ONE

(Your score will be either 0 or 10) **Your Score**

ROUND 3: WONDERWALL

(Maximum Score = 20) **Your Score**

ROUND 4: MEMORY WONDERWALL

(Maximum Score = 20) **Your Score**

TOTAL SCORE

HOLIDAY SCORE

Go to the Holiday Prize Table on page 5 to find out whether your total score will take you around the world!

Game Twelve

Answers for Game Twelve on page 159. Scorecard page 125.

1 The Winning Line

HOW TO PLAY

First answer the following six questions in the spaces provided (Tip! Answers will be a number). Transfer your answers to the oval spaces in the Winning Line. If these answers add up to the winning number, you have a Winning Line! There is no time limit for this round.

1 If you add up the number of US presidents whose surnames have been Bush, Roosevelt and Adams, how many do you get?

2 If all the Angels in 'Captain Scarlet and the Mysterons' met all the men who have walked on the Moon, how many people would there be?

3 Add together the 'Night' on which Christmas decorations are traditionally taken down, to the number of coins in the fountain in a Frank Sinatra song?

4 Add up the number of football league clubs from Nottingham, Derby and Sheffield: how many are there in total?

5 What number is obtained by multiplying the number of times the banns should be read before a wedding, by the number of times a week the Guardian newspaper is published?

6 If the number of sides of a hexagon is subtracted from those of a nonagon, how many sides remain?

Create your Winning Line:

+ + + + +

= Winning Number = 64

SCORING

Score one point for each question answered correctly, plus an additional two points if your answers successfully add up to the Winning Number.

2 Looking After Number One

HOW TO PLAY

Look at the following ten questions. Tick only those questions whose answers correspond with the winning number shown in the oval below the questions. There is no time limit for this round.

For example, if the Winning Number = 7

How many dwarfs lived with Snow White?

1 To the nearest whole number, at how many revolutions per minute does a long-playing vinyl record spin?

2 According to the Bible, for how many days did the rains of the Great Flood fall?

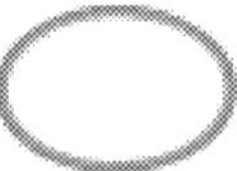

3 King Edward VIII abdicated in 19...?

4 At what temperature on the Fahrenheit scale does pure water freeze?

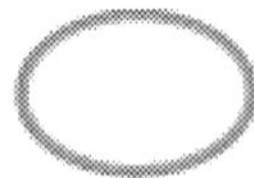

5 When playing cribbage, what number must players not exceed when laying out their cards?

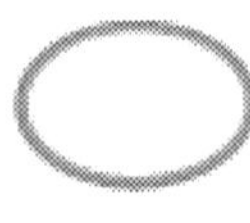

6 What is the minimum age at which a person is eligible to be elected President of the USA?

7 In horse-racing parlance, the odds known as 'double carpet' are ... to 1?

8 How many days are there in five weeks?

9 On a standard clock face, how many degrees are there between each number?

10 On a regulation soccer pitch and measured in feet, how far is the penalty spot from the centre of the goal line?

WINNING NUMBER = 

SCORING

Score ten points if your answers match exactly with those in the back of the book.

3 Wonderwall

13 Nottinghamshire
34 Brandy
28 Snickers
5 Malaria
29 Aristotle
32 James
40 Argentina
10 Eponymous
11 Pythagoras
19 Bacardi
14 Lion
30 Hampshire
45 Bounty
22 Brother
1 India
15 Sister
48 Henry
26 Unanimous
25 Archimedes
44 Copper
7 Kent
33 Anonymous
18 Guatemala
2 Chlorine

1 For which county does England fast bowler Darren Gough play?

2 The main printed circuit board of a computer is sometimes called the ...board?

3 Who is the Safety Inspector at the Springfield nuclear power station?

4 In 1789, Captain William Bligh was cast adrift from which ship, after some of the crew mutinied?

5 In which country is the Golden Temple at Amritsar?

6 Which spirit is one of the ingredients of a 'Rusty Nail' cocktail?

7 What is the name of the first monarch to be both King of England and Scotland?

8 What does the first 'M' stand for in the MMR vaccination?

9 Which chemical element has the symbol C?

10 What word means everybody is in agreement?

HOW TO PLAY AND SCORING

The answers to the questions are in the Wonderwall below. Write the number of your answer in the space provided, crossing answers off the Wall as you go. The time limit is 3 minutes. One point for each correct answer.

3 Homer
43 Charles
20 Carbon
42 Synonymous
49 Cobalt
21 William
12 Edward
46 Whisky
36 Venezuela
35 Somerset
27 Measles
23 Father
24 Galaxy
8 Mother
38 Auntie
37 Socrates
17 Chile
16 Chromium
31 Migraine
41 Myxomatosis
47 Mars
6 Vodka
4 Mumps
39 Yorkshire
9 Rum

11 The three-times winner of the Aintree Grand National is Red ...?

12 The actress who plays Molly MacDonald in 'Monarch of the Glen' is Susan ...?

13 What is added to water supplies as a disinfectant?

14 Who formulated the theorum which states that the square of the hypotenuse of a right angled triangle is equal to the sum of the squares of the other two sides?

15 Complete the name of the organization founded in the USA in 1935, 'Alcoholics ...'?

16 The name of which disease is derived from the Italian for 'bad air'?

17 Which chocolate bar was re-advertised in 2002 with the slogan 'Pleasure you can't measure'?

18 Complete the title of the 1977 UK No 1 by Julie Covington, 'Don't Cry For Me, ...'?

19 What is the first name of the youngest son of Queen Elizabeth II?

20 What family relation is sometimes applied affectionately to the BBC?

4 Memory Wonderwall

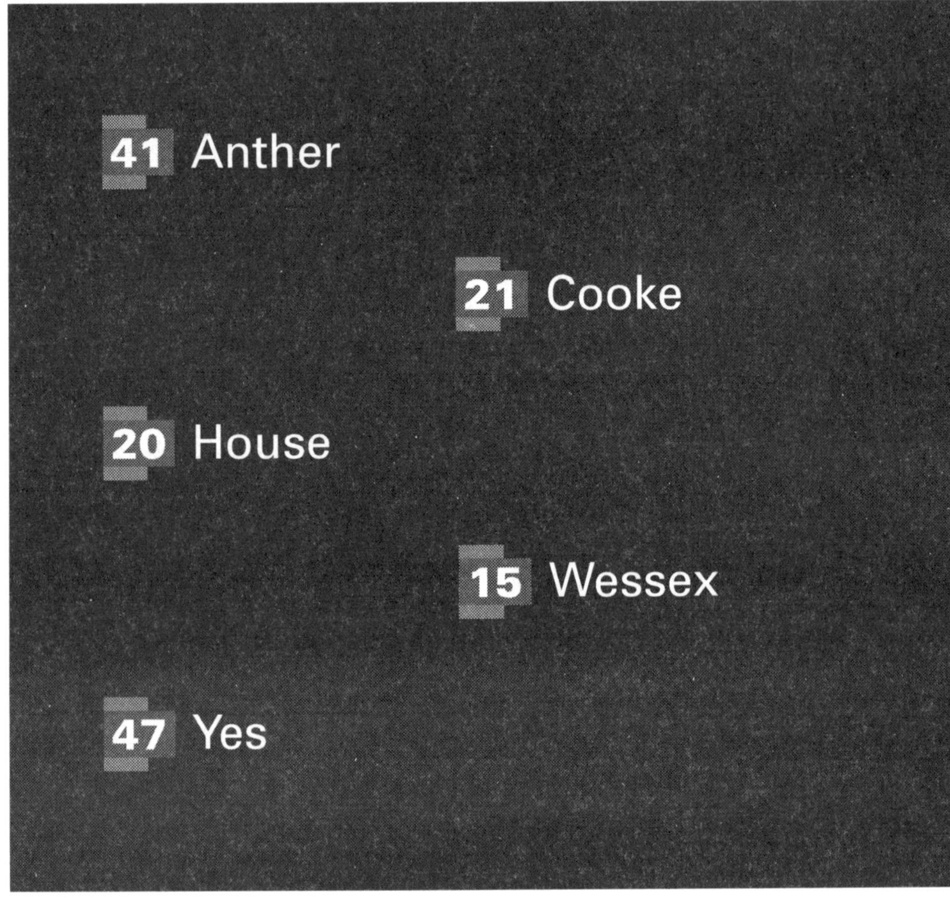

HOW TO PLAY

You have one minute to memorise the mini Wonderwall! Memorise both the word answer and its corresponding number. Then turn the page to answer the ten questions from memory.

FOR EXAMPLE

Question: What is the capital of Iceland?

Answer: 11. Reykjavik (*Scores 2 points*)

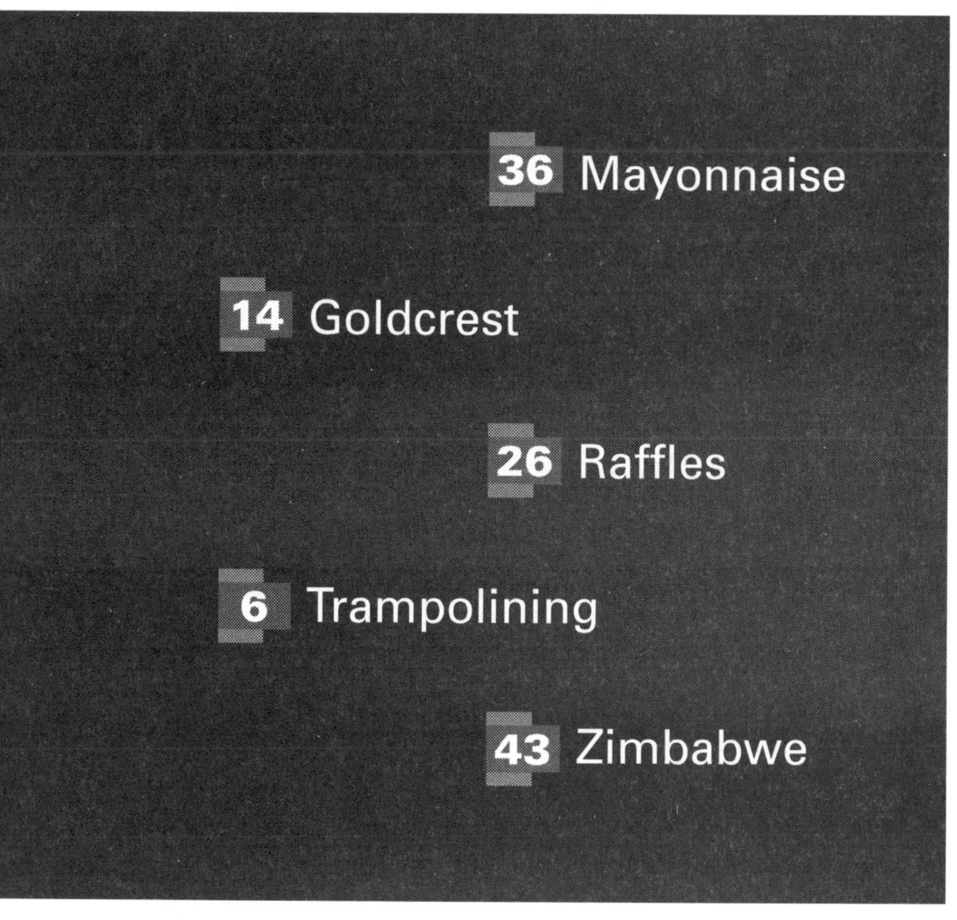

SCORING

Award yourself one point for answering the question correctly, and a bonus point for remembering the number that corresponds to your answer.

Turn page for questions

Round 4: Memory Wonderwall Questions

1 Which band was formed in 1968 by Jon Anderson, Chris Squire, Tony Kaye, Bill Bruford and Peter Banks?

2 Which gentleman thief was created by E W Hornung?

3 In which sport might a competitor perform an 'adolph' or a 'randolph'?

4 Who has delivered his 'Letter from America' on British radio since 1946?

5 What is the smallest native bird of the British Isles?

6 Bulawayo is a town in which country?

7 What is 'Howard's End', in the title of the film and book?

8 Which dressing takes its name from the capital city of the island of Minorca?

9 Alfred the Great ruled which Saxon kingdom?

10 What name is given to the part of a flower's stamen that produces the pollen?

Scorecard

Answers for Game Twelve are on page 159.

ROUND 1: THE WINNING LINE

Number of correct answers ---------

Add 2 points for creating the Winning Line ---------

(Maximum Score = 8) **Your Score**

ROUND 2: LOOKING AFTER NUMBER ONE
(Your score will be either 0 or 10) **Your Score**

ROUND 3: WONDERWALL
(Maximum Score = 20) **Your Score**

ROUND 4: MEMORY WONDERWALL
(Maximum Score = 20) **Your Score**

TOTAL SCORE

HOLIDAY SCORE

Go to the Holiday Prize Table on page 5 to find out whether your total score will take you around the world!

GAME THIRTEEN

Answers for Game Thirteen on page 159. Scorecard page 135.

1 The Winning Line

HOW TO PLAY

First answer the following six questions in the spaces provided (Tip! Answers will be a number). Transfer your answers to the oval spaces in the Winning Line. If these answers add up to the winning number, you have a Winning Line! There is no time limit for this round.

1. If you subtract the date in March of St Patrick's Day from that in November of St Andrew's Day, what number do you get?

2. If Harry Potter spent 1½ years in each of the houses at Hogwarts School, how many years would he be there?

3. Add the number of times the letter 'I' appears in Mississippi to the number of times the letter 'A' appears in Australia?

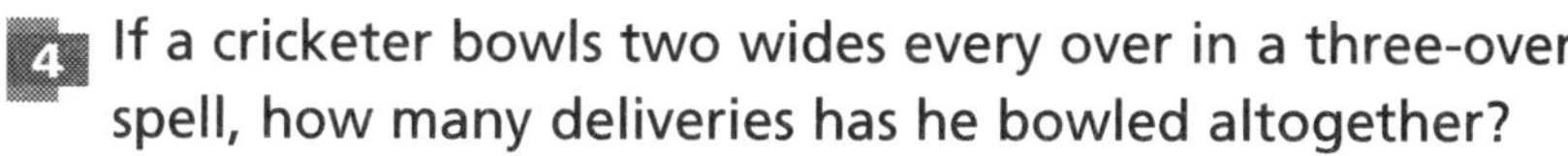

4 If a cricketer bowls two wides every over in a three-over spell, how many deliveries has he bowled altogether?

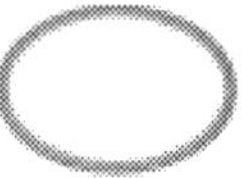

5 If Lady Jane Grey had reigned for a fortnight longer, how many days would she have been queen of England?

6 If a car drives at a constant 20mph, how many miles will it have travelled in 45 minutes?

Create your Winning Line:

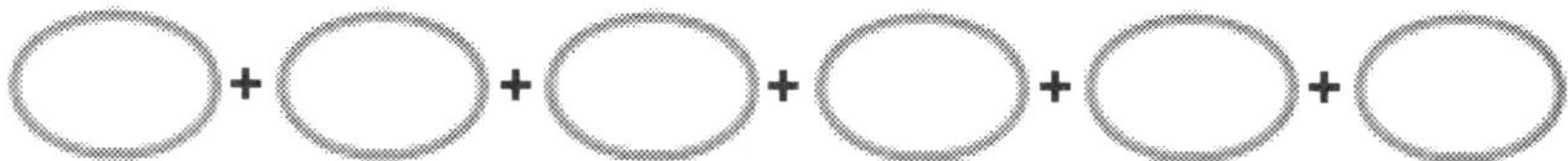

= Winning Number = 88

SCORING

Score one point for each question answered correctly, plus an additional two points if your answers successfully add up to the Winning Number.

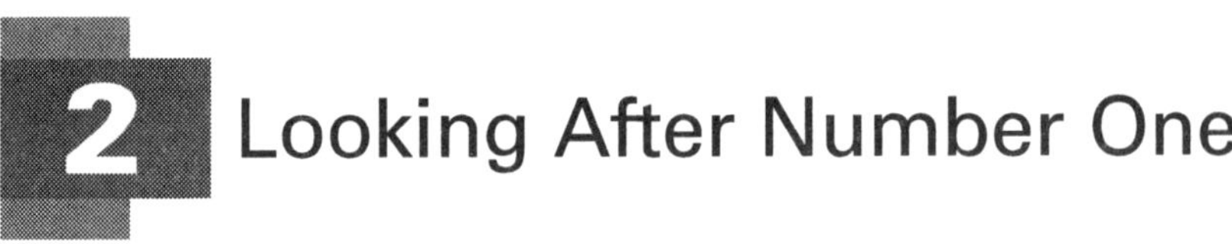

2 Looking After Number One

HOW TO PLAY

Look at the following ten questions. Tick only those questions whose answers correspond with the winning number shown in the oval below the questions. There is no time limit for this round.

For example, if the Winning Number = 7

How many dwarfs lived with Snow White?

1 How many counties are there in the Republic of Ireland?

2 What is the number of the motorway linking London to Folkestone?

3 What is the lowest number that cannot be scored with one dart on a standard trebles dartboard?

4 In pounds, what is the value of the banknote that has featured Sir Edward Elgar on the back?

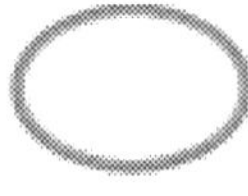

5 Which number is zwanzig in German?

6 In Imperial weights and measures, how many ounces make up 1½ pounds?

7 How many players are there in an Australian Rules football team?

8 The postcode for Albert Square in 'EastEnders' is E...?

9 According to the popular song, at what age do you get 'the key to the door'?

10 Alcock and Brown became the first people to fly across the Atlantic Ocean nonstop in 19...?

WINNING NUMBER = 

SCORING

Score ten points if your answers match exactly with those in the back of the book.

3 Wonderwall

13 Swan
34 Aquarius
28 Silver
5 Semaphore
29 Tinkerbell
32 Weekly
40 Lotto
10 Morse
11 Thumbelina
19 Leo
14 Coot
30 Philippines
45 Taiwan
22 Ophelia
1 Olive
15 Drake
48 Octavia
26 Aldis
25 Duck
44 Goldilocks
7 Javelin
33 Motto
18 Pisces
2 Golden

1 A pair of fish is normally used to represent which sign of the Zodiac?

2 In the cartoon world, what is the name of Popeye's girlfriend?

3 How often is an AGM held?

4 What colour is associated with the name of the most famous bridge in San Francisco Bay?

5 According to the children's story, who visited the home of the Three Bears?

6 Java and Bali are two islands of which country?

7 The men's world record for which athletics field event is the longest in distance?

8 Which form of signalling involves the use of two flags?

9 Which British steam locomotive holds the world speed record of 126 mph, set in 1938?

10 To what did the UK National Lottery change its name in May 2002?

HOW TO PLAY AND SCORING

The answers to the questions are in the Wonderwall below. Write the number of your answer in the space provided, crossing answers off the Wall as you go. The time limit is 3 minutes. One point for each correct answer.

3 Gemini
43 Blotto
20 Monthly
42 Thailand
49 Olympia
21 Flash
12 Cinderella
46 Jet
36 Rapunzel
35 Grotto
27 Olivia
23 Discus
24 Aries
8 Daily
38 Vietnam
37 Indonesia
17 Fortnightly
16 Caber
31 Tic-tac
41 Hammer
47 Mallard
6 Copper
4 Yearly
39 Bronze
9 Shot

11 ◯ John Thaw played which TV detective?

12 ◯ What word goes before 'Telegraph' and 'Mail' to give two national newspapers?

13 ◯ What is an informal slang word for being very drunk?

14 ◯ Who got her prince after the glass slipper fitted?

15 ◯ Which NASA space programme preceded the Apollo programme?

16 ◯ Which country was previously known as Formosa?

17 ◯ Who, according to folk-history, continued playing bowls whilst the Spanish Armada approached the English coast?

18 ◯ Which prehistoric 'Age' followed the Stone Age and preceded the Iron Age?

19 ◯ In Shakespeare's 'Hamlet', which character goes mad and drowns?

20 ◯ King Edward I of England was known as the ' ... of the Scots'?

4 Memory Wonderwall

16 China

9 Mushroom

4 Stripping

27 Molecule

32 Puissance

HOW TO PLAY

You have one minute to memorise the mini Wonderwall! Memorise both the word answer and its corresponding number. Then turn the page to answer the ten questions from memory.

FOR EXAMPLE

Question: What is the capital of Iceland?

Answer: 11. Reykjavik (*Scores 2 points*)

SCORING

Award yourself one point for answering the question correctly, and a bonus point for remembering the number that corresponds to your answer.

Turn page for questions

Round 4: Memory Wonderwall Questions

1 In chemistry, what name is given to the smallest part of a compound that exhibits the properties of that compound?

2 What was the nickname of the US General Thomas Jackson?

3 In which 1942 film were Ronald Reagan and Ann Sheridan originally cast in the lead roles?

4 Piranhas are native to the rivers of which continent?

5 Taiwan lies off the coast of which other country?

6 What name is given to the specialist high jump event in show jumping?

7 What type of food is a morel?

8 'Look At Me, I'm Sandra Dee' is a song from which stage and screen musical?

9 What term is used in TV for the showing of a programme at the same time on every day of the week?

10 The 'Beat Generation' was a literary movement founded in which decade?

Scorecard

Answers for Game Thirteen are on page 159.

ROUND 1: THE WINNING LINE

Number of correct answers ---------

Add 2 points for creating the Winning Line ---------

(Maximum Score = 8) **Your Score**

ROUND 2: LOOKING AFTER NUMBER ONE

(Your score will be either 0 or 10) **Your Score**

ROUND 3: WONDERWALL

(Maximum Score = 20) **Your Score**

ROUND 4: MEMORY WONDERWALL

(Maximum Score = 20) **Your Score**

TOTAL SCORE

HOLIDAY SCORE

Go to the Holiday Prize Table on page 5 to find out whether your total score will take you around the world!

GAME FOURTEEN

Answers for Game Fourteen on page 159. Scorecard page 145.

1 The Winning Line

HOW TO PLAY

First answer the following six questions in the spaces provided (Tip! Answers will be a number). Transfer your answers to the oval spaces in the Winning Line. If these answers add up to the winning number, you have a Winning Line! There is no time limit for this round.

1 In the USA, how many quarters would you receive in change if you paid for a $6.25 item with a $10 note?

2 If Rome had been built on one less hill, on how many would it now stand?

3 If one of the teams on 'University Challenge' had a player missing, how many students would be taking part?

4 If you need one more railway station for the set when playing 'Monopoly', how many do you already have?

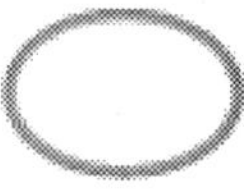

5 How many pockets are there on five full-size snooker tables?

6 Theoretically, how many times could you compete in the famous Le Mans race in three weeks?

Create your Winning Line:

( ) + ( ) + ( ) + ( ) + ( ) + ( )

= Winning Number = 82

SCORING

Score one point for each question answered correctly, plus an additional two points if your answers successfully add up to the Winning Number.

2 Looking After Number One

HOW TO PLAY

Look at the following ten questions. Tick only those questions whose answers correspond with the winning number shown in the oval below the questions. There is no time limit for this round.

For example, if the Winning Number = 7

How many dwarfs lived with Snow White?

1 Moving outwards from our Sun, which number planet is Uranus?

2 If you are in a dangerous position or at a disadvantage, you are said to be behind which numbered pool ball?

3 According to the saying, after how many years of marriage does the 'itch' begin?

4 In 1954, Roger Bannister became the first person to run a mile in under how many minutes?

5 How many were 'Magnificent' in the title of the classic 1960 western?

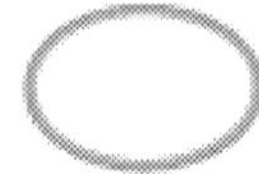

6 'Thou shalt not kill' is which number of the Ten Commandments?

7 When established in 1957, how many countries formed the Common Market?

8 What number do the opposite sides of a dice add up to?

9 The prefix 'mega' indicates that a number has been raised by 10 to the power of ...?

10 What 'o'clock' is the shadow on a man's face when he is ready for another shave?

WINNING NUMBER = 

SCORING

Score ten points if your answers match exactly with those in the back of the book.

3 Wonderwall

13 Arm
34 Golf
28 Berkeley
5 Carter
29 Foot
32 Triangle
40 Ricardo
10 Knee
11 Tennis
19 Rugby
14 Neck
30 Glazier
45 Badminton
22 Pedro
1 Luxembourg
15 Russell
48 Bricklayer
26 Cylinder
25 Los Angeles
44 Nixon
7 Thigh
33 Plumber
18 Clinton
2 Lisbon

1. Who succeeded Reagan as president of the USA?
2. With which sport is the Fijian Vijay Singh chiefly associated?
3. The name of which city is used in the NATO alphabet as a codeword for the letter 'L'?
4. Mint sauce is the traditional accompaniment to which meat?
5. In which part of the body is the bone called the ulna?
6. What was the name of the inept waiter in 'Fawlty Towers'?
7. Who, on a building site, is most likely to use a hod?
8. What is the home of a rabbit called?
9. In which London square is Nelson's Column?
10. What geometric figure might be described as scalene, isosceles or equilateral?

HOW TO PLAY AND SCORING

The answers to the questions are in the Wonderwall below. Write the number of your answer in the space provided, crossing answers off the Wall as you go. The time limit is 3 minutes. One point for each correct answer.

3 Bush
43 Luxor
20 Lamb
42 Cone
49 Tiler
21 Lodge
12 Bloomsbury
46 Warren
36 Calf
35 Cricket
27 Lima
23 Drey
24 Venison
8 Pike
38 Figaro
37 Form
17 Thatcher
16 Leicester
31 Miguel
41 Sett
47 Fish
6 Manuel
4 Ford
39 Trafalgar
9 Rhombus

11 ◯ Where would you be flying to if your luggage tag read 'LAX'?

12 ◯ The name of which professional is derived from the Latin for 'lead'?

13 ◯ What does a piston fit into inside in a car engine?

14 ◯ What was 'invented' by William Webb Ellis in 1823?

15 ◯ What was the name of the early 20th century 'Group' that included Virginia Woolf?

16 ◯ What was the name of Dennis Waterman's character in 'The Sweeney'?

17 ◯ What is the small gatehouse at the entrance to a large country house or park called?

18 ◯ Where will you have a swelling if you are suffering from a goitre?

19 ◯ Who provided a UK No 1 for Brotherhood of Man in 1978?

20 ◯ In 1987, which BBC weatherman famously said there was no hurricane approaching the UK?

4 Memory Wonderwall

34 Nougat

18 Ridgeley

45 Conquistadors

2 Rebecca

29 Host

HOW TO PLAY

You have one minute to memorise the mini Wonderwall! Memorise both the word answer and its corresponding number. Then turn the page to answer the ten questions from memory.

FOR EXAMPLE

Question: What is the capital of Iceland?
Answer: 11. Reykjavik (*Scores 2 points*)

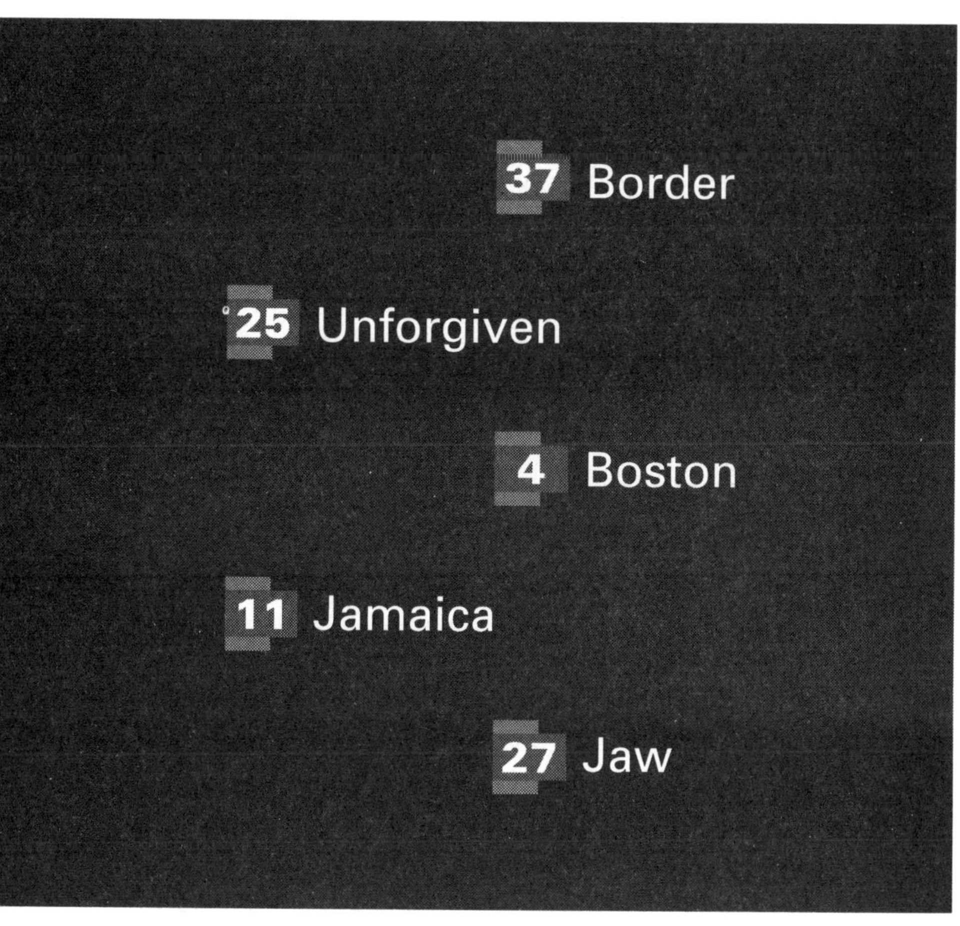

SCORING

Award yourself one point for answering the question correctly, and a bonus point for remembering the number that corresponds to your answer.

Turn page for questions

Round 4: Memory Wonderwall Questions

1 Which independent television company is based in Carlisle?

2 From which US city do the 'Celtics' basketball team come?

3 What specific term defines what a parasite lives upon?

4 Which Spanish name was given to the conquerors of South America?

5 For which film did Clint Eastwood win his first Best Director Oscar?

6 Which novel opens with the line, 'Last night I dreamt I went to Manderley again'?

7 What was the surname of George Michael's partner in Wham!?

8 Montélimar in France is best known for the production of what type of chewy sweet?

9 Montego Bay is a resort on which Caribbean island?

10 What part of an insect's anatomy is its mandible?

Scorecard

Answers for Game Fourteen are on page 159.

ROUND 1: THE WINNING LINE

Number of correct answers ---------

Add 2 points for creating the Winning Line ---------

(Maximum Score = 8) **Your Score**

ROUND 2: LOOKING AFTER NUMBER ONE

(Your score will be either 0 or 10) **Your Score**

ROUND 3: WONDERWALL

(Maximum Score = 20) **Your Score**

ROUND 4: MEMORY WONDERWALL

(Maximum Score = 20) **Your Score**

TOTAL SCORE

HOLIDAY SCORE

Go to the Holiday Prize Table on page 5 to find out whether your total score will take you around the world!

GAME FIFTEEN

Answers for Game Fifteen on page 159. Scorecard page 155.

1 The Winning Line

HOW TO PLAY

First answer the following six questions in the spaces provided (Tip! Answers will be a number). Transfer your answers to the oval spaces in the Winning Line. If these answers add up to the winning number, you have a Winning Line! There is no time limit for this round.

1 What is left if you divide the number of Heinz 'Varieties' by Paul Hardcastle's 1985 UK No 1 single?

2 In 'Sing a Song of Sixpence', if the cook had used only half as many blackbirds in the pie, how many would there have been?

3 If the government brought St George's Day forward by two days, on what date in April would it be celebrated?

4 In a golf tournament, if you complete two rounds and then retire injured, how many holes have you played?

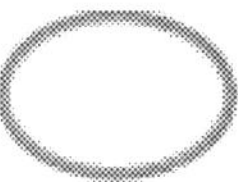

5 If the number of countries that border Portugal is added to the number that border Denmark, what number do you have?

6 In the Morse Code SOS distress call, how many dots remain if you take away all the dashes?

Create your Winning Line:

( ) + ( ) + ( ) + ( ) + ( ) + ( )

= Winning Number = 80

SCORING

Score one point for each question answered correctly, plus an additional two points if your answers successfully add up to the Winning Number.

2 Looking After Number One

HOW TO PLAY

Look at the following ten questions. Tick only those questions whose answers correspond with the winning number shown in the oval below the questions. There is no time limit for this round.

For example, if the Winning Number = 7

How many dwarfs lived with Snow White?

1 If CII is divided by III, what is the answer in Arabic numerals?

2 In the UK, what is the minimum age at which someone may supervise a learner driver?

3 During a game of rugby union, how many players are normally on the pitch at any time?

4 How many cubic feet make up one cubic yard?

5 How many days are there in the month of June?

6 In England and Wales, a baby must be registered within how many days of its birth?

7 Queen Elizabeth II's real birthday falls on which date in April?

8 How many teams competed in the final stages of the 2002 FIFA World Cup?

9 How many years of marriage are celebrated by a pearl anniversary?

10 Adolf Hitler became Chancellor of Germany in 19...?

WINNING NUMBER = 

SCORING

Score ten points if your answers match exactly with those in the back of the book.

3 Wonderwall

13 Egg
34 Poland
28 Lug
5 Sheffield
29 Vincent
32 Geronimo
40 Calf
10 Buttercup
11 Colt
19 Finland
14 Victor
30 Nut
45 Switzerland
22 Banana
1 Minnehaha
15 Manchester
48 Glasgow
26 Bristol
25 Thistle
44 Pocahontas
7 Edinburgh
33 Mug
18 Ear
2 Rose

1 What is the first name of Mr Meldrew, played on TV by Richard Wilson?

2 What is the predominant flavouring of the drinks Ouzo and Pernod?

3 In which city does the 'Old Firm Derby' football match take place?

4 Which native American princess allegedly saved John Smith, an English colonist, from being killed?

5 What term applies to a favoured competitor in a tournament who is expected to reach the later stages?

6 What name is given to a small, powerful boat used for towing larger vessels, especially in a harbour?

7 What is the national emblem of Scotland?

8 Where, in the human body, is there a membrane called the tympanum?

9 What name is given to a young rabbit, beaver or ferret?

10 'Suomi' appears on the stamps of which European country?

HOW TO PLAY AND SCORING

The answers to the questions are in the Wonderwall below. Write the number of your answer in the space provided, crossing answers off the Wall as you go. The time limit is 3 minutes. One point for each correct answer.

3 Virgil
43 Strawberry
20 Stomach
42 Tug
49 Vaughan
21 Cochise
12 Bug
46 Kidney
36 Liver
35 Bulb
27 Cub
23 Orange
24 Kit
8 Daffodil
38 Romania
37 Seed
17 Bulgaria
16 Spore
31 Shamrock
41 Hiawatha
47 Heart
6 Aniseed
4 Lemon
39 Vernon
9 Jug

11 ◯ What word can be used for a small insect, a miniature microphone or an error in a computer program?

12 ◯ Which Royal Navy destroyer was sunk by an Exocet missile in May 1982?

13 ◯ With which plant is St Patrick said to have illustrated the doctrine of the Holy Trinity?

14 ◯ Which of the Tracy brothers is the regular pilot of Thunderbird 2?

15 ◯ Transylvania is a region of which country?

16 ◯ What was the surname of Samuel, who patented the revolver pistol in the 1830s?

17 ◯ Whose name was adopted by American paratroopers during WWII, and shouted when they jumped from their aircraft?

18 ◯ From which part of a cow is tripe obtained?

19 ◯ In the nursery rhyme, what is Humpty Dumpty usually perceived to be?

20 ◯ One of the members of the boy band Take That was Jason ...?

4 Memory Wonderwall

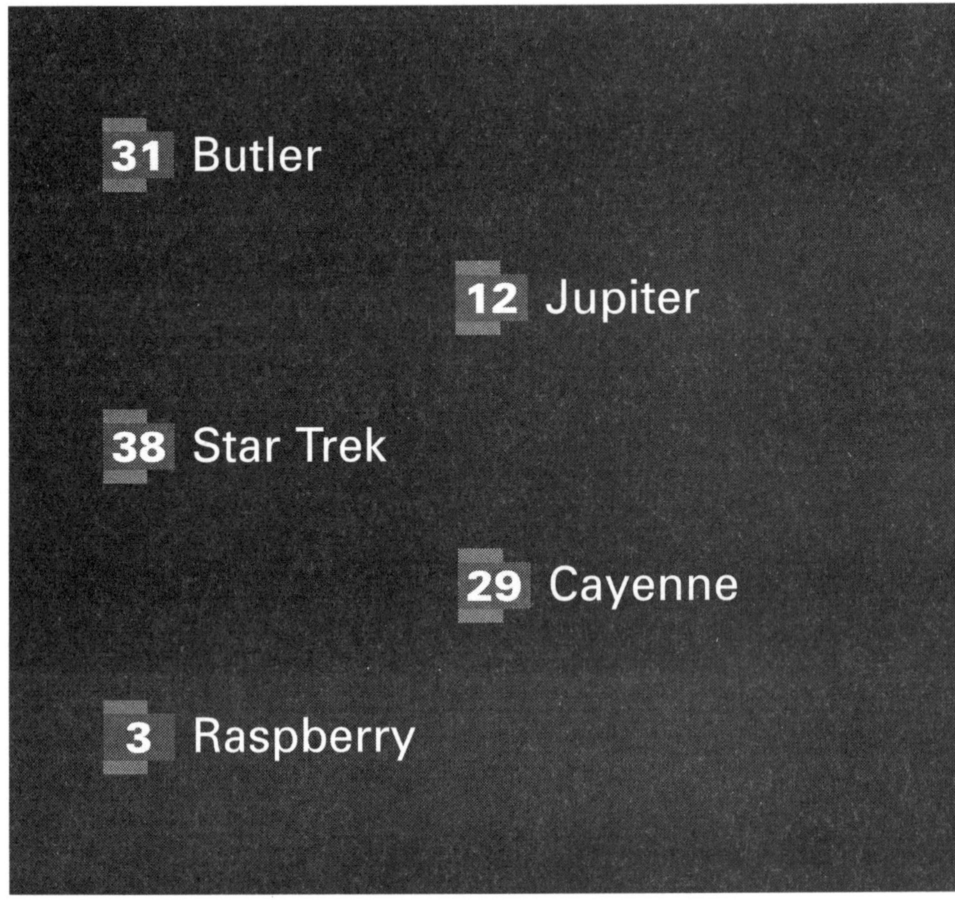

HOW TO PLAY

You have one minute to memorise the mini Wonderwall! Memorise both the word answer and its corresponding number. Then turn the page to answer the ten questions from memory.

FOR EXAMPLE

Question: What is the capital of Iceland?

Answer: 11. Reykjavik (*Scores 2 points)*

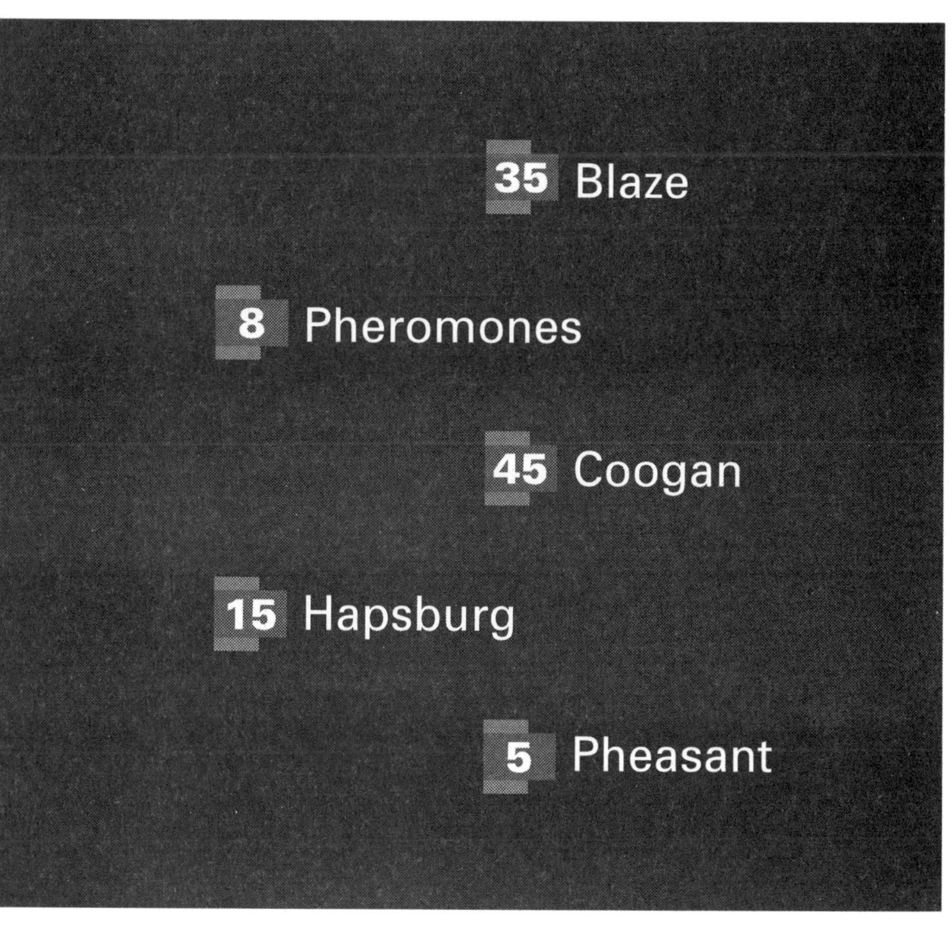

SCORING

Award yourself one point for answering the question correctly, and a bonus point for remembering the number that corresponds to your answer.

Turn page for questions

Round 4: Memory Wonderwall Questions

1 What is the light marking on a horse's face known as?

2 Which dynasty ruled the Austro-Hungarian Empire?

3 What is the profession of 'The Admirable Crichton' in the book of the same name?

4 What name is given to the substances secreted by certain animals that influence the behaviour of other animals?

5 Which shooting season runs from October 1st to February 1st?

6 Which fruit forms the basis of a Melba sauce?

7 Which pepper shares its name with the capital of French Guiana?

8 Which comedian created the characters Paul and Pauline Calf and Tony Ferrino?

9 What popular name is given to Mozart's Symphony No. 41?

10 'The Undiscovered Country' was the final film in a series featuring the original cast of which TV series?

Scorecard

Answers for Game Fifteen are on page 159.

ROUND 1: THE WINNING LINE

Number of correct answers ---------

Add 2 points for creating the Winning Line ---------

(Maximum Score = 8) **Your Score**

ROUND 2: LOOKING AFTER NUMBER ONE

(Your score will be either 0 or 10) **Your Score**

ROUND 3: WONDERWALL

(Maximum Score = 20) **Your Score**

ROUND 4: MEMORY WONDERWALL

(Maximum Score = 20) **Your Score**

TOTAL SCORE

HOLIDAY SCORE

Go to the Holiday Prize Table on page 5 to find out whether your total score will take you around the world!

THE ANSWERS

GAME ONE

Round One – The Winning Line
7 + 5 + 4 + 1 + 6 + 2 = 25 Winning Number
Round Two – Looking After Number 1
Winning Number = 4. Correct questions: 2, 6, 7
Round Three – Wonderwall
1: 41 Aberdeen, 2: 34, Leopard 3: 17 White, 4: 10 Liver, 5: 13 William, 6: 11 Red, 7: 4 Perth, 8: 46 Trent, 9: 16 Galliano, 10: 14 Polish, 11: 7 Mouse, 12: 49 Harrier, 13: 19 Swiss, 14: 26 Rat, 15: 44 Dee, 16: 45 Advocaat, 17: 28 Lion, 18: 47 Nimrod, 19: 22 Heart, 20: 15 Edward
Round Four – Memory Wonderwall
1: 18 Chicago, 2: 31 Speedway, 3: 47 Godfrey, 4: 26 Venus, 5: 16 Crete, 6: 44 Resurrection, 7: 24 Saki, 8: 3 Rossini, 9: 42 Boar, 10: 21 Bucket

GAME TWO
Round One – The Winning Line
8 + 5 + 15 + 8 + 15 + 2 = 53 Winning Number
Round Two – Looking After Number 1
Winning Number = 2. Correct questions: 1, 3, 6, 8
Round Three – Wonderwall
1: 34 Jupiter, 2: 3 Silver, 3: 45 London, 4: 38 Tchaikovsky, 5: 46 Oliver, 6: 47 Raven, 7: 40 Rum, 8: 48 Trombone, 9: 41 Michigan, 10: 24 Diamond, 11: 17 Turner, 12: 25 Cornet, 13: 18 Copper, 14: 11 Tennessee, 15: 4 Beethoven, 16: 39 Neptune, 17: 7 Melbourne, 18: 49 Sapphire, 19: 42 Brandy, 20: 10 Swan
Round Four – Memory Wonderwall
1: 27 Hybrid, 2: 43 Canadian, 3: 23 Avocet, 4: 12 Chocolate, 5: 41 Lacrosse, 6: 20 Enya, 7: 49 Switzerland, 8: 38 Gormenghast, 9: 18 Spain, 10: 46 Hollyoaks

GAME THREE

Round One – The Winning Line
9 + 18 + 10 + 10 + 16 + 3 = 66 Winning Number
Round Two – Looking After Number 1
Winning Number = 10. Correct questions: 1, 2, 5, 6
Round Three – Wonderwall
1: 4 Robin, 2: 46 Ceylon, 3: 39 Knight, 4: 32 Brazil, 5: 25 Dracula, 6: 23 Frog, 7: 42 Velvet, 8: 35 Apollo, 9: 28 Blue, 10: 26 Sergeant, 11: 19 China, 12: 12 Newt, 13: 5 Peru, 14: 47 Eagle, 15: 22 Corporal, 16: 40 Gemini, 17: 33 Zombies, 18: 24 Cotton, 19: 17 Red, 20: 10 Castle
Round Four – Memory Wonderwall
1: 11 Caesar, 2: 27 USA, 3: 6 Harvey, 4: 32 French, 5: 48 Counterpoint, 6: 15 Mauritius, 7: 41 Scurvy, 8: 8 Everton, 9: 36 Llewelyn, 10: 13 Okra

GAME FOUR

Round One – The Winning Line
35 + 11 + 28 + 7 + 16 + 3 = 100 Winning Number
Round Two – Looking After Number 1
Winning Number = 21. Correct questions: 3, 10
Round Three – Wonderwall
1: 37 Nebuchadnezzar, 2: 35 Quart, 3: 27 Darwin, 4: 28 Poison, 5: 21 Othello, 6: 30 Thames, 7: 38 Stimulated, 8: 31 Blue, 9: 24 Raven, 10: 17 Baker, 11: 10 Super, 12: 18 Methuselah, 13: 11 Chandler, 14: 20 Yellow, 15: 13 Canberra, 16: 46 Shannon, 17: 39 Tweed, 18: 47 Magpie, 19: 48 Cleopatra, 20: 26 Gill
Round Four – Memory Wonderwall
1: 39 Wales, 2: 6 Flamingo, 3: 32 Tasman Sea, 4: 48 El Cid, 5: 28 Tungsten, 6: 17 Ghost, 7: 46 Willow, 8: 25 Salmon, 9: 5 Piccalilli, 10: 43 Darling

GAME FIVE

Round One – The Winning Line
4 + 7 + 6 + 9 + 28 + 18 = 72 Winning Number
Round Two – Looking After Number 1
Winning Number = 25. Correct questions: 1, 3, 4, 10
Round Three – Wonderwall
1: 20 Blair, 2: 13 Capri, 3: 45 St Ives, 4: 38 Suez, 5: 44 Penny, 6: 27 Richard, 7: 48 Zebra, 8: 41 Fitzgerald, 9: 6 Apple, 10: 28 September, 11: 16 Kiel, 12: 9 Fitzsimmons, 13: 31 Thatcher, 14: 26 November, 15: 19 Newmarket, 16: 12 Fiesta, 17: 33 George, 18: 10 Tanner, 19: 40 Avocado, 20: 39 Wildebeest
Round Four – Memory Wonderwall
1: 36 Snowball, 2: 16 Wampum, 3: 42 Chesapeake, 4: 9 Jumanji, 5: 25 Ulysses, 6: 2 Carrot, 7: 18 Zimbabwe, 8: 46 Natural, 9: 23 Cement, 10: 39 Prague

GAME SIX

Round One – The Winning Line
8 + 5 + 14 + 16 + 7 + 4 = 54 Winning Number
Round Two – Looking After Number 1
Winning Number = 1. Correct questions: 4, 5, 6, 7, 8
Round Three – Wonderwall
1: 6 Bacon, 2: 14 Bottom, 3: 7 Paris, 4: 49 SAS, 5: 47 Pluto, 6: 40 Horseradish, 7: 33 Sweden, 8: 26 Ireland, 9: 18 Stork, 10: 9 Capricorn, 11: 12 Finland, 12: 5 CIA, 13: 3 Mint, 14: 45 Banger, 15: 15 Taurus, 16: 8 Madrid, 17: 48 Oberon, 18: 34 Duck, 19: 27 Jupiter, 20: 4 Lindisfarne
Round Four – Memory Wonderwall
1: 9 Cecil, 2: 35 Jupiter, 3: 2 Lentils, 4: 31 Fluff, 5: 8 Gorillas, 6: 24 Highgate, 7: 39 J, 8: 16 Macbeth, 9: 32 Muirfield, 10: 12 Prince

GAME SEVEN

Round One – The Winning Line
12 + 17 + 13 + 3 + 15 + 5 = 65 Winning Number
Round Two – Looking After Number 1
Winning Number = 6. Correct questions: 3, 5, 7, 9
Round Three – Wonderwall
1: 37 Library, 2: 32 Joey, 3: 25 Ruby, 4: 30 Cardiff, 5: 13 Jack, 6: 19 Sneezed, 7: 12 Derbyshire, 8: 7 Tuesday, 9: 42 Pig, 10: 38 Circle, 11: 31 Bathroom, 12: 36 Northern, 13: 45 Willie, 14: 40 Porcupine, 15: 6 Hiccuped, 16: 27 Queen, 17: 20 Lancashire, 18: 23 Belfast, 19: 44 Thursday, 20: 49 Emerald
Round Four – Memory Wonderwall
1: 18 Coventry, 2: 34 Toothpaste, 3: 1 Swimming, 4: 27 Dawson, 5: 43 Lewes, 6: 22 Heart, 7: 48 China, 8: 15 Montana, 9: 44 Haddock, 10: 21 Platypus

GAME EIGHT

Round One – The Winning Line
7 + 8 + 24 + 30 + 1 + 3 = 73 Winning Number
Round Two – Looking After Number 1
Winning Number = 16. Correct questions: 2, 3, 4, 6, 8
Round Three – Wonderwall
1: 5 Japan, 2: 7 Mustard, 3: 48 Wellington, 4: 46 Hood, 5: 16 Snail, 6: 9 Dutch, 7: 2 Voice, 8: 26 Blue, 9: 19 Institution, 10: 12 Chequers, 11: 21 Cow, 12: 29 French, 13: 22 Hearing, 14: 31 Trunk, 15: 24 Edinburgh, 16: 41 Red, 17: 11 Iodine, 18: 43 Vinegar, 19: 36 Pakistan, 20: 37 Checkers
Round Four – Memory Wonderwall
1: 25 Casino, 2: 2 Larkin, 3: 18 Arthritis, 4: 47 Rookery, 5: 24 Pretenders, 6: 40 Tokyo, 7: 7 Spinach, 8: 33 Kiki, 9: 12 Staffordshire, 10: 28 Canada

GAME NINE

Round One – The Winning Line
3 + 27 + 39 + 9 + 8 + 10 = 96 Winning Number
Round Two – Looking After Number 1
Winning Number = 12. Correct questions: 2, 4, 10
Round Three – Wonderwall
1: 32 Spain, 2: 9 Patella, 3: 2 Inch, 4: 44 Panther, 5: 19 Resolution, 6: 12 Colon, 7: 5 Rome, 8: 47 Cricket, 9: 45 Aquarius, 10: 30 Violin, 11: 23 Mile, 12: 24 Badminton, 13: 17 Revolution, 14: 10 Italy, 15: 3 Bracket, 16: 27 Piano, 17: 20 Paris, 18: 13 Bear, 19: 6 Virgo, 20: 4 Radius
Round Four – Memory Wonderwall
1: 12 Danegeld, 2: 40 Trombone, 3: 30 Costa Brava, 4: 9 Wolverhampton, 5: 25 Elk, 6: 2 Billy Bunter, 7: 18 Hovis , 8: 47 Nun, 9: 24 Metronome, 10: 19 Hesitation

GAME TEN

Round One – The Winning Line
19 + 10 + 1 + 12 + 4 + 21 = 67 Winning Number
Round Two – Looking After Number 1
Winning Number = 40. Correct questions: 1, 2, 3, 9
Round Three – Wonderwall
1: 19 Spaghetti, 2: 12 Nurse, 3: 5 Harold, 4: 47 Calcutta, 5: 45 Comets, 6: 38 Baines, 7: 31 Jagger, 8: 24 Pride, 9: 17 White, 10: 25 Germany, 11: 18 William, 12: 11 Burnley, 13: 4 Macaroni, 14: 2 Asteroids, 15: 36 Anger, 16: 29 Bombay, 17: 30 Georgia, 18: 23 Greene, 19: 16 Baker, 20: 9 Juggler
Round Four – Memory Wonderwall
1: 48 Avon, 2: 28 Pregnant, 3: 5 Weather, 4: 21 Jeffreys, 5: 37 Radiohead, 6: 14 Almond, 7: 30 Collector, 8: 9 Okapi, 9: 35 Nancy , 10: 2 Krajicek

GAME ELEVEN

Round One – The Winning Line
21 + 19 + 7 + 13 + 2 + 10 = 72 Winning Number
Round Two – Looking After Number 1
Winning Number = 48. Correct questions: 2, 9, 10
Round Three – Wonderwall
1: 29 Hexagon, 2: 22 Sting, 3: 4 Green, 4: 46 Chelsea, 5: 3 Simple, 6: 47 Turkey, 7: 40 Heel, 8: 33 Saffron, 9: 1 Federal, 10: 43 Derby, 11: 36 Prang, 12: 8 Chicken, 13: 39 Nottingham, 14: 11 Easy, 15: 16 Pentagon, 16: 9 Field, 17: 35 Arsenal, 18: 18 Ginger, 19: 17 Finger, 20: 38 Jet
Round Four – Memory Wonderwall
1: 16 Benvolio, 2: 32 Yak, 3: 9 Macedonia, 4: 25 Ethiopia, 5: 4 Cassiopeia, 6: 30 Test card, 7: 46 Netball, 8: 26 Brigadoon, 9: 5 Vodka, 10: 44 Philadelphia

GAME TWELVE

Round One – The Winning Line
6 + 17 + 15 + 5 + 18 + 3 = 64 Winning Number
Round Two – Looking After Number 1
Winning Number = 36. Correct questions: 3, 10
Round Three – Wonderwall
1: 39 Yorkshire, 2: 8 Mother, 3: 3 Homer, 4: 45 Bounty, 5: 1 India, 6: 46 Whisky, 7: 32 James, 8: 27 Measles, 9: 20 Carbon, 10: 26 Unanimous, 11: 9 Rum, 12: 30 Hampshire, 13: 2 Chlorine, 14: 11 Pythagoras, 15: 33 Anonymous, 16: 5 Malaria, 17: 47 Mars, 18: 40 Argentina, 19: 12 Edward, 20: 38 Auntie
Round Four – Memory Wonderwall
1: 47 Yes, 2: 26 Raffles, 3: 6 Trampolining, 4: 21 Cooke, 5: 14 Goldcrest, 6: 43 Zimbabwe, 7: 20 House, 8: 36 Mayonnaise, 9: 15 Wessex, 10: 41 Anther

GAME THIRTEEN

Round One – The Winning Line
13 + 6 + 7 + 24 + 23 + 15 = 88 Winning Number
Round Two – Looking After Number 1
Winning Number = 20. Correct questions: 2, 4, 5, 8
Round Three – Wonderwall
1: 18 Pisces, 2: 1 Olive, 3: 4 Yearly, 4: 2 Golden, 5: 44 Goldilocks, 6: 37 Indonesia, 7: 7 Javelin, 8: 5 Semaphore, 9: 47 Mallard, 10: 40 Lotto, 11: 10 Morse, 12: 8 Daily, 13: 43 Blotto, 14: 12 Cinderella, 15: 3 Gemini, 16: 45 Taiwan, 17: 15 Drake, 18: 39 Bronze, 19: 22 Ophelia, 20: 41 Hammer
Round Four – Memory Wonderwall
1: 27 Molecule, 2: 43 Stonewall, 3: 10 Casablanca, 4: 36 South America, 5: 16 China, 6: 32 Puissance, 7: 9 Mushroom, 8: 24 Grease, 9: 4 Stripping, 10: 30 1950s

GAME FOURTEEN

Round One – The Winning Line
15 + 6 + 7 + 3 + 30 + 21 = 82 Winning Number
Round Two – Looking After Number 1
Winning Number = 7. Correct questions: 1, 3, 5, 8
Round Three – Wonderwall
1: 3 Bush, 2: 34 Golf, 3: 27 Lima, 4: 20 Lamb, 5: 13 Arm, 6: 6 Manuel, 7: 48 Bricklayer, 8: 46 Warren, 9: 39 Trafalgar, 10: 32 Triangle, 11: 25 Los Angeles, 12: 33 Plumber, 13: 26 Cylinder, 14: 19 Rugby, 15: 12 Bloomsbury, 16: 5 Carter, 17: 21 Lodge, 18: 14 Neck, 19: 38 Figaro, 20: 47 Fish
Round Four – Memory Wonderwall
1: 37 Border, 2: 4 Boston, 3: 29 Host, 4: 45 Conquistadors, 5: 25 Unforgiven, 6: 2 Rebecca, 7: 18 Ridgeley, 8: 34 Nougat, 9: 11 Jamaica, 10: 27 Jaw

GAME FIFTEEN

Round One – The Winning Line
3 + 12 + 21 + 36 + 2 + 6 = 80 Winning Number
Round Two – Looking After Number 1
Winning Number = 30. Correct questions: 3, 5, 9
Round Three – Wonderwall
1: 14 Victor, 2: 6 Aniseed, 3: 48 Glasgow, 4: 44 Pocahontas, 5: 37 Seed, 6: 42 Tug, 7: 25 Thistle, 8: 18 Ear, 9: 24 Kit, 10: 19 Finland, 11: 12 Bug, 12: 5 Sheffield, 13: 31 Shamrock, 14: 3 Virgil, 15: 38 Romania, 16: 11 Colt, 17: 32 Geronimo, 18: 20 Stomach, 19: 13 Egg, 20: 23 Orange
Round Four – Memory Wonderwall
1: 35 Blaze, 2: 15 Hapsburg, 3: 31 Butler, 4: 8 Pheromones, 5: 5 Pheasant, 6: 3 Raspberry, 7: 29 Cayenne, 8: 45 Coogan, 9: 12 Jupiter, 10: 38 Star Trek